Now Go Home

Now Go Home

Wilderness, Belonging, and the Crosscut Saw

Ana Maria Spagna

Oregon State University Press
Corvallis

The paper in this book meets the guidelines for permanence and durability of the Committee on Production Guidelines for Book Longevity of the Council on Library Resources and the minimum requirements of the American National Standard for Permanence of Paper for Printed Library Materials Z39.48-1984.

Library of Congress Cataloging-in-Publication Data
Spagna, Ana Maria.
  Now go home : wilderness, belonging, and the crosscut saw / Ana Maria Spagna.
    p. cm.
  ISBN 0-87071-009-5 (alk. paper)
1. Spagna, Ana Maria. 2. United States. National Park Service.—Officials and employees—Biography. 3. National parks and reserves—West (U.S.) 4. Lesbians—United States—Biography. 5. Washington (State)—Biography. I. Title.
  CT275.S5995 A3 2004
  333.78′3′092—dc22

                                    2003024636

Oregon State University Press
101 Waldo Hall
Corvallis OR 97331-6407
OREGON STATE
UNIVERSITY   541-737-3166 • fax 541-737-3170
http://oregonstate.edu/dept/press

Contents

Now Go Home

Wilderness, Homelessness, and the Crosscut Saw

Usually in these woods, on the long dark access trails along the river valleys, there is no choice: it's either drizzle or bugs. Today there are both. Bridget and I have been left behind by the crew on this, the last and best tour of the year. It should have been a brief detour to saw a medium-sized log lying perpendicular across the trail. An hour. Two at most. But this is a particularly stubborn hemlock, the tree most likely to pinch the crosscut saw and refuse to allow the steel teeth to drag across the grain. I once worked a hemlock for seven days straight. That's what worries me.

I take the wooden handle in my gloved hand, and pull back steadily, resisting the temptation to muscle the thing, to yank with all my frustrated might. On the other side of the hemlock, Bridget cradles her handle without resistance until my arm extends completely. Then she pulls. Two, four, six jerky strokes before the saw lurches again and stops.

"Don't pull down," Bridget says.

"I'm not pulling down," I say, believing without arguing that she is the one pulling down.

We wrestle with our handles, trying to jiggle the saw loose, then take the dull pulaski—half-axe, half-hoe—we have been hauling with us for this eight-day tour and chip away at the wood hugging the blade, careful not to chop too close. Eventually the saw releases, and we reposition ourselves in silence to try again.

When Congress enacted the Wilderness Act in 1964, three years before I was born, they left for me, the "future generation" that is the mainstay of all environmental rhetoric, a boon and a loophole.

No mechanized anything would be allowed in capital W Wilderness. No cars. No bikes. No wheelbarrows even. And no chainsaws. Except, of course, for administrative purposes. The National Park Service, the federal agency created by and for urban conservationists, chose to keep their hiking constituents happy, and chainsaws raged through park trails unhindered by the pesky new legislation. The United States Forest Service, ironically, the agency of clear-cut logging, stuck to the intent and spirit of the law. If conservationists wanted Wilderness, by golly they'd get it. Sure, we'd still maintain the trails, but we'd do it—get this—with crosscut saws. It was the stuff of comedy, they must have thought.

"You've got the best job in the world."

Two hikers approach, a couple maybe in their early fifties, and greet us with the most common sentiment that we hear.

Bridget wipes the sweat from her forehead with a grimy glove, leaving a swipe of mud across her brow, and grins. I scowl. I don't mean to scowl. The hikers have been out in the same bug drizzle that we have. But I am tired. The muscles beneath my right shoulder blade feel, with every stroke, as if they are being bludgeoned with a dull axe. I need to switch hands more often.

"Do you mind if we take your picture?" the gentleman asks.

"Sure," Bridget cries. She hops to her feet and pulls off her kerosene-stained wool shirt. She rolls back the sleeve of her T-shirt to expose her bicep. Bridget is my size, about five foot four, and her Arnold Schwarzenegger pose leaves the hikers in stitches, as it did the hikers before them, and the ones before them.

The gentleman turns to me, awaiting my pose, or at least hoping I will grab the other saw handle for an action shot. Instead, I turn and tromp over the jungle of ferns to squat in the dark forest. From here I can hear the interrogation:

"Where are you from? Do you do this all year? What do you do the rest of the year?"

Bridget's voice is even and patient. Chicago. No, we'll be laid off in a month or so. Never know what winter will bring.

"Well, thanks," the woman says earnestly. "Thank you for clearing the trail for us."

I watch Bridget nod, smile. She offers a hand to each of the hikers as they struggle to fit a boot toe between the thick grooves in the bark and clamber up and over the troublesome hemlock. Each of them lands gracefully on the other side. They are fit, it seems, and eager to be out for a lengthy trek in these drippy woods. My self-pity is shameful.

My job is part choice and part trap. My first summer after college I volunteered in a national park and discovered a secret. The government will pay you to live in the Wilderness, not for a weekend or a two-week vacation, but for six, eight months at a time. It is grueling and satisfying work. You can spend eight ten-hour days in a row clearing the thick overgrown ferns and berry brambles that obscure a trail. Then you can look back and see the open swath stretching out below as the trail takes you up and out of the woods. You can tell yourself: that's it, that's what I did this week.

But it's not a sure thing. Every spring when you call to ask about the summer, there is a barrage of ifs to deal with: if the budget is in, if the division is still funded, if the high country has melted out. Then they offer a job, the same job usually from the year before, no security, not great pay, but the chance to spend another season sleeping on the soft duff of fir needles with the roar of a river at your back and rugged glacier peaks above.

I sometimes tell myself that the conviction to stay is altruism, a desire to keep the trails open for hikers. Or maybe it's some version of Deep Ecology, laying down my life for the Wilderness piece by piece (a reconstructed knee here, a trick back there) rather than chaining myself in front of bulldozers. Mostly it's selfishness. The decision to stay is always made at the moment when the ground freezes hard and trail work is over for another season. We are left at the mercy of that other wilderness: Interstate Five, Bellevue Square Mall. We buy new clothes, rehearse old manners, and fly in a matter of hours over spaces that would take months to cover on foot.

My arm now complains enough that I can only make it about twenty strokes without a break. I hold the saw handle in both my fists, brace my feet against the hemlock again, and lean back, trying to use my back instead of my traitor right shoulder. Seventeen, eighteen, nineteen. Rest.

In the early part of this century only simple skills were required to be a forest ranger: dig a line around a forest fire, build a cable bridge, tie a diamond hitch, use a crosscut, sharpen a crosscut. Today the permanent rangers, the office folks, have college degrees and computer terminals. They're necessarily skilled in ecosystem management, budget manipulation, conflict resolution. Only seasonal laborers dig line, build bridges, use crosscuts. And even we have no need for a diamond hitch since the mules in our district were retired after Reagan left office. The Reagan administration had demanded record harvests, frantic clear-cutting that left the Forest Service rich in blood money with which to fund other divisions: wildlife biology, watershed protection, wilderness management. When Spotted Owl lawsuits halted logging, trail budgets were halved, then quartered. No more money for mules, and without them we spend much of our time lugging equipment through the woods, less time actually working. Every spring, map companies call to ask which trails to delete for lack of maintenance.

Eventually, Bridget and I manage to pound a plastic wedge into just the right spot to open the cut a hair. I pull the near-empty liter of kerosene from my pack and pour a little across the blade for lubrication, then take my handle again. For a moment, steel teeth skate across the grain and deposit pungent tailings in a perfect cone over the mud. The saw buzzes like it does only when we've got it right, when we're completely in synch, when we have rhythm.

"What are you thinking about?" Bridget asks.

"What?"

"When you're sawing, what do you think about?"

I can't think of a thing. Seven, ten, thirty hours of skilled mindlessness.

"Nothing," I say.

"Me either," Bridget says.

If we were truly altruistic, or even realistic, we'd sneak in the chainsaw to speed up the process. We do it sometimes, half-jog past the Wilderness boundary sign with a chainsaw conspicuously slung over one shoulder. We act righteous, reminding ourselves that we owe it to the public to open the trails, that we're saving the government hours of our wages, that the Park Service, like the privileged kid next door, gets to use chainsaws so we should too. The truth is that we're tense, though we don't admit it. We're afraid of getting caught, of course, in the unlikely case that one of the permanent rangers might wander by, but we're also afraid of the precedent. There's danger in it. If it's this easy to eliminate the crosscut, to accelerate the pace and conform for the sake of efficiency, we could be the next to go. Then where would we be?

Missoula, Eugene, Seattle, Moab, Flagstaff. I map my unemployed, underemployed winters zigzagging between the Rockies and the Pacific. Packing, driving, reading, mending, sitting. Glorious sitting. It's retirement, real early retirement, I joke to my friends. But winter requires ingenuity. One winter I slept in friends' extra bedroom, paying rent by baking bread each morning at dawn before facing the job search. Imagine how the applications look: thirty-five jobs in fifteen years. None longer than six months.

"How long are you committed to stay?" an employer might ask.

"I'm a good worker," I'd say, "really good."

↷

Bridget and I finish sawing the hemlock by headlamp. We lie down on our backs on the damp earth to try to push the round we have cut off the trail with our legs. We position our feet against it with our knees to our chests.

"One, two, three ..." We count off and push with all the might of our ten-mile-a-day quads. Nothing. The tree must have embedded itself in the ground with the force of its fall sometime last winter. We stand and begin to search in the dark for a sturdy fir limb from the forest floor to use to lever the round up. I hold onto the end of the branch, and Bridget positions herself directly in front of me.

"One, two ..." I pull down on the end of the branch while Bridget stuffs rocks under the log to hold it up. Lever and rock, lever and rock. I begin to lose patience, put my back into the effort to try to lever a few extra inches, and snap off the end of the branch. I stumble backwards in the dark.

"You OK?" Bridget asks without looking at me. She repositions the lever to try again.

ᐸᕬ

The next morning we are on our way out, at last, to the trailhead as rare fall sunlight spills between the red orange leaves of vine maple, yellow alder. For ten miles, the trail follows the river, a raging torrent of blue gray glacial silt. I look up to see the early dusting of snow on the peaks, the long shadows across the valley, and I feel the air cool my neck beneath my wool cap. This is my favorite feeling, this shameless end-of-the-week, end-of-the-season exhaustion buzz. I'm watching for wild huckleberries on the side of the trail, feeling the air fill my lungs, walking effortlessly with my eight-day pack, the long saw wrapped in used fire hose and slung under the shoulder strap, resting across my fingers, my fingers going numb. I'm fretting over how soon I'll be out of shape, how softness will encroach. I'm thinking, like I do every year, about maybe stashing food and a tent for winter camping up here, or about settling in the drizzly logging town below, to stay put, to spend the winter collecting unemployment, waiting for spring. I shift the weight of my pack and close my eyes for a moment, fighting the sadness of leaving.

Bridget approaches me from behind. "What are you thinking about?" she asks.

"Ice cream," I lie, "and clean sheets."

Late fall will settle in this valley, comforting and unnerving as an early evening nap, heavy rain splattering dully on a blanket of leaves. The highway will close, and hunters will race back to the city in shiny 4x4s, dead elk draped across bedliners. My leather boots will shrink beside the woodstove, and I will return to splitting alder bucked quickly and efficiently with the new Husqvarna chainsaw in the shed. NPR will drone in the background about deficits and budget reductions, computers buzzing with the chatter of a New Age. With one last cup of coffee before I drive, I'll look up at the crosscut saw mounted above the television at a local diner, a Vermont farmhouse painted over its rusty teeth. From where I sit, it will look exactly like hope.

Now Go Home

We loved that song. We learned it in our size 6X bikinis, our bare feet blistering on the concrete deck of Susie Beckwith's built-in pool: *I wish they all could be ...* Oh, we were. We were. And how we relished it, diving off the edge, splashing, submerging, and springing high off the very bottom of the deep end. Over and over. Then dancing together in rehearsed bikini formation: *I wish they all could be ...* Comparing our Coppertone buns as a matter of pride during a childhood in paradise. *California Girls.*

And Susie Beckwith was my very best friend: the tallest, the smartest, and of course, the prettiest. Even though I weighed less: fifty-four instead of fifty-eight. We weighed ourselves daily, then lay out in the sun with the transistor radio between us. Every twenty minutes, the DJ told us to turn. And we did. We rode two-wheelers out into the field, the open weedy block between our cul de sac and the Catholic school, rode over the hard-packed jumps and trails while the sun set fiery red behind silhouetted palms. We played awash in the last of the light, blond reflecting orange, and dry grass rustling in the wind, crushing like crepe paper under our bike tires. When the streetlights came on, we collapsed in the den at her house or mine. And on TV, the sun set fiery red behind the palms at the Bradys' house too.

Sunset in the Pacific Northwest is far less flamboyant. Either clouds or mountains obscure it. I sit bundled in three muddy shirts and workboots drinking Schmidt's, the animal beer, in the Spar Tree, a backwoods tavern eighty miles northeast of Seattle. The Spar Tree is an anomaly, a bikers' bar in a loggers' town, a place where outsiders can fit in. It was the only place where my trail

crew, all men besides me, felt comfortable enough to watch the
NBA playoffs, and I came along for the company. But as day seeps
into night without drama, the guys start reminiscing about their
childhoods, and I avoid the conversation. I glance, by instinct,
around the bar and shift uncomfortably on my stool. It is not
paranoia. It's just the truth. There are things you don't do in a tavern
up here, even the Spar Tree: You don't wear sandals. You don't
cheer for the Jazz. You don't admit, ever, that one day not long-
enough ago, you climbed in the passenger seat of an Oldsmobile
and moved north. From that other state.

Later came the other song. *Plenty of room at the Hotel* … Yes, that
too. Plenty. Subdivisions sprouting pell-mell; new floor plans
leveling jumps and trails; sprinkler systems soaking the hard-pack.
As if me and Susie could care. We preferred the beach and pestered
our parents to drive us to Laguna, forty-five minutes or three hours
from home, depending on traffic.

We loved the lifeguard, Mike Murphy. He told us his name and
slipped us his phone number. Oh God, was he cute. We played
this game: Jump over the waves. Jump over the waves. We drifted
out into wide spiraling riptides that dragged us out further, past
where our parents could see. And we only had one rule: never
never never turn back. One day, Mike Murphy had to rescue us
three times.

Truth is, I don't give a damn about basketball. I am tired and
sore from a day of early-season tree-planting work—stepping and
sliding down a steep clear-cut littered with the sooty slash from
last fall's burn. The unit has been cut too often, so this time we
were told not to plant a new crop for harvest, just some willows to
hold the hillside from sliding down into the river below. We spent
the day grubbing out narrow trenches, shoving cuttings into the
slop, and tromping back to the top for more. I am growing happily
inebriated and increasingly distracted. Above the diveted slab of
fir that serves as the bar, the Spar Tree sports a red and white banner:
"Snohomish County's Number Two Vender of Schmidt's." Number

Two? I turn the icy can, a twenty-two ouncer, in my palm. When in Rome. And I turn my attention to the growing crowd that seems to have caught the contagious expectancy of the big game. They are well dressed in fresh leather and shiny boots, and fidgety. Mostly, they are numerous. Every few minutes another bike roars into the lot.

"Check her out." Kevin, my normally reserved foreman, has forgotten the mixed company long enough to ogle the girl in a beer commercial.

It's fifty degrees outside, and it's been raining on and off for about six months, and on the big screen a nearly naked blond is playing beach volleyball. The guys, quite apparently, are aroused. Me, I'm trying to be disgusted, but it comes out homesick. This is what gets to me, and it's common enough, I know. You can't go home again. Not you, not me, not anyone. But my betrayal was worse, I convince myself, because it's my own, of course, and because it feels so much like a general conspiracy. The Bradys, the Beach Boys, Mike Murphy, tanned and sculpted to impish extremes, they conspired to make us believe that we Californians were the chosen ones, living at the center of the universe. Only over time, and in varying amounts, did we realize that our home was not paradise and that our loyalty, like that of the too-eager freshmen at a pep rally, was naive and laughable.

"Find the quiet place in your heart where Jesus lives," whispered our high school religion teacher to the class. A former nun with a cereal-bowl haircut and sensible sandals, she was a caricature so familiar to us, the children of the seventies, that we could not even bear to ridicule her. "Share with Him your innermost feelings," she said. And we obeyed.

Reagan was president, too. The same dilemma. Aging and so obviously ignorant, he seemed beyond reproach, a too-easy target. We groaned when we watched him, like we groaned when we watched scratchy films in religion class where earnest unshaven types rocked to the sounds of guitar Mass hymns. We were embarrassed, sure, but we were well behaved, and rather than attack the icons we inherited, we immersed ourselves in pop culture, the only security we knew. Boys wore ties to school by choice. Girls wore tartan plaid. Thick soupy air poisoned the palm fronds while everyone listened on Walkmen to super-coiffed British bands like Flock of Seagulls, like Duran Duran. The betrayal dawned on me slowly, amidst the clatter of lockers and the mumbled offers of cocaine: I was done dreamin' about my home state.

In my deepest heart, where Jesus lived temporarily, I began to long for trees as escape. Not trees themselves—I'd seen too few to know—but the idea of trees, like the idea of the big city to a small-town kid. It was a seventies dream recast, the back-to-nature bit. Too many Mountain Dew commercials for me. Too much John Denver. There was a picture book of the Northwest I read to my goddaughters, the toddlers of close family friends, that showed radiant green rolling hills. That's where I was headed. I doodled fir trees on my Pee Chee folders and ran cross-country through orange groves, the only trees I could find. I ran slowly, horribly, losing every race.

Susie submerged more easily. She moved lithely through the thick smog, tried out for cheerleading, drove an orange Super Beetle with specialized tags: "SUZYSOJ." She was elected Miss Moreno Valley, a crime-drenched suburb of our suburb. I went to the contest wearing blocky pumps and pearls, brought flowers even. I might have wished to rebel, to wear a punk-rock T-shirt, maybe, and roll my eyes, had I ever seen anyone do such a thing. Or maybe just to laugh. But these were not options.

Sex was, of course, an option. I had my first orgasm in Moreno Valley, which used to be called Sunnymead, but which me and Susie called Scummymead before she became Queen. They built Scummymead up with model homes like movie sets, like they were supposed to be real. Shoddy, I guess you'd say, but huge. They built a multiplex theater and a Kings Table restaurant beside the interstate. I never understood why people would stop there after racing across the Mohave. Hollywood was just a little further west, then the Pacific. Moreno Valley was nothing, I thought at the time. It was on the way to something, maybe, but it was nothing.

But I'm one to talk. I stopped in Scummymead every afternoon in senior year to romp around with our history teacher, a too-skinny and shameless man fifteen years older than me. The chosen day arrived months before I graduated to his first name. I lay waiting, anxious and bored, on the floor while he adjusted the needle on the turntable and rechecked the drapes. He had bought a 45 for the occasion, an REO Speedwagon single: *I can't fight this feeling*. He lay down beside me and pulled me against him so tightly that the knot of his loosened tie dug into my breastbone. He had, he must have figured, three minutes to get the job done, but I was sturdy and patient, blinded by a single-minded greedy curiosity. We had to restart the music three or four times.

In the sweaty relief that followed, Mr. History pulled off his fogged eyeglasses, and I saw in his eyes the same rich blue of giddy possibility that I sometimes imagined seeing on the smogless horizons of winter. I buried my face snugly into the hollow below his collarbone, and let myself sink into a love more fierce and inevitable, perhaps, than my California dreams had ever been. He held me there for a long time.

☙

"It used to be paradise."

Back at the Spar Tree, Kevin is bemoaning the fact that a new brew pub is going up in Everett, thirty miles to the west. It's a common complaint, how we gotta find a new place. The wait for the ferries across to the Olympic peninsula grows longer every day: forty-five minutes or three hours, depending on traffic. Quik Lubes and coffee carts creep over farmlands. Housing prices skyrocket. Taxes soar. Kevin is passionate on the subject. He claims he will not continue to live in a county once it has a brew pub.

"Maybe Montana?" someone suggests.

I understand their frustration. It's not that we can't go home again, they say, but that we can run as far as we want and there we are. Every Starbucks the same. Every cereal aisle a Xerox copy. Every tavern complaint exactly like the rest. Even mine.

๛

The circumstance was common enough. Precocious girl. Predatory man. But even now that I am the age that he was then, I cannot so easily unmuddy my own story. I was headed to the University of Oregon, only months from leaving, and I was separating myself by measure from loyalties that had the power to paralyze me. I didn't know I was using him. I fell headlong and shifted my passion a half step from a place I'd never seen to a man I'd never know. When, sometime in the middle of summer, Mr. History decided to follow me north, the two passions wed. For long enough.

We drove through endless tall dark firs, tracking the highway signs to the university. Finally having arrived, we pulled up beside a late model Jeep Cherokee with a popular bumper sticker: "Welcome to Oregon: Now Go Home." I laughed. I had dreamed of making the place home for so long. And I knew the rule: never never never turn back. I forced Mr. History to pull over and snap a photo of me beside the Cherokee, while I pretended to be Mary Tyler Moore, spinning with glee and tossing my hat into the air.

Mr. History did not laugh. The rain, the bumper sticker, the whole situation oppressed him, I think. He cowered in the two-bedroom apartment he rented, in part, on advances from my scholarship money, convinced that no one would hire him. He bought pillow-sized bags of bright yellow popcorn and six-packs of Coke and watched Laker games on TV with pathetic longing. I rode my bike to and from school and returned in the rain to nuzzle his stubbled whiskers, to circle the want ads, to burn fish sticks for dinner. I stared, sometimes, from across the room into the darkened lenses of his new light-sensitive eyeglasses, wishing for a glimpse of blue. Then I'd give up and try to talk him into going out, anywhere. But he would not leave his ratty Goodwill recliner.

Eventually, he turned back. He pocketed a hefty chunk of the scholarship cash and drove south on a gloomy Superbowl Sunday. I watched the Oldsmobile taillights trail off past the Now Go Home Cherokee parked in the same place where it had been when we arrived, parked in the same place always. Then I wandered across campus to leave a post-it note on a professor's desk explaining that I had to go back home to California.

The professor, a no-nonsense woman who had already gone to great lengths to encourage my lackluster studies, caught me sneaking through the dank hallway and dragged me by the arm to her office.

"Four seconds," she announced. She slammed the office door.

I stood confused, gazing out in my sad puppy trance across the main campus square, a deep brooding green. Not radiant at all.

"That's the longest an orgasm can last. Four seconds." She had an unwavering glare. "Get over it," she said.

"How'd you know it was because of …?"

"It always is," she said. "Now, get over it."

I wouldn't show my shock. I sank more deeply into the puppy gaze, offended vaguely and embarrassed certainly, playing the innocent Catholic schoolgirl. Outside, the eternal drizzle turned silently and miraculously into something else. It was the first time I'd seen such a thing. Snow on the ground, sure. Snow that you drive to the mountains to see. But never coming down.

"OK," I said. "OK."

She marched out of the office, and I stood alone for a moment watching big feathery flakes crisscross the gray. Then I left and jogged circles through the snowy streets in my too-thin sweatshirt, stumbling home finally to the empty apartment.

I continued to run, growing stronger over months, years, following trails of sawdust among dormant blackberry vines along the Willamette. Even bought a rainjacket. Still too thin. When I grew tired, I collapsed in the soggy grass to stare up into the sky. Drizzle splattered off my cheeks, soaked through my jacket. On the Walkman, Cat Stevens goaded me on: *If you want to be free, be free.* Oh, I was. I was.

And I learned to lie. In taverns and elsewhere. Where are you from? Just say Eugene. Skip the high-school section on the job application. It's a dead giveaway. Avoid conversations about family vacations or anything further back than, say, three years, then five, then ten. Measure the distance and nurture the disdain.

"Or Idaho? Or maybe northwestern Colorado?" an old-timer, a local postman, leans in closer, to make room for even more bikers, and to help Kevin navigate memory and fantasy in search of a home. I scoot my own stool a few inches down the bar, feeling downright claustrophobic. I have downed too many Schmidts, and I am growing annoyed by this migration angst. If growth is inevitable, then how much, and when to stop, and when to move on? It's all so very mucky. It seems to me that the Northwest today, like the California of my youth, is, well, youthful: indestructible, full of itself, blinded by a greedy curiosity. Four seconds. That's the longest it can last.

"Get over it," I interrupt. It's the first thing I've said all night.

Kevin turns toward me, silent and angry. He knows my secret and he's about to use it like a weapon, I know. Tell me how I've Californicated the place. And I will tell him I didn't Californicate anybody. Maybe myself, I'll say. But no one else. Just as he calculates if and how best to respond to me, the jukebox in the back room blares loudly enough to drown us out.

Goodbye, Norma Jean, though I never knew you at all.

It's not Elton John. That's for sure. Kevin and I turn in unison to see a biker, leather adorned and sentimental, repeating what few lyrics he can recall, mostly the opening line, over and over, into a microphone.

Goodbye, Norma Jean …

Karaoke night at the Spar Tree. Later the story will be exaggerated to mythic around-the-campfire proportions. But there's a moment, a very brief moment, before we succumb to hysterics, when the Spar Tree falls still, and we're all listening.

Uh, Goodbye …

The biker's voice might be slurry, and his song cloying, but there's not a person who doesn't know how he feels. For the first time in years, I remember my history teacher with something like affection. Goodbye is, I realize, as poignant as it is common. And even disdain can pass.

❧

These days I drive home more often. The place has changed. Banners drape across the garage doors of Spanish-style homes. Call 525-REPO. Car models hover in the early nineties, not shiny enough.

On my last trip, I piled Mom's collection of pop cans into the back of my pickup; this is our environmental truce, that she'll save the cans if I'll take them down to the Lucky supermarket and stuff them in the Cash for Cans machine that crunches them one at a very slow time. I stood alone in the Lucky parking lot, soaking in the dry heat rising off the pavement like a remedy. Cash for Cans wouldn't take crushed cans, inexplicably wouldn't take others. A scratched bar code? An off-brand? No saying. In the distance the San Bernardino Mountains hid behind the familiar cloak of what Mom insistently calls haze. The machine added two and a half pennies for each can it accepted. Shove and reposition. Sugar flies and god knows what on my hands. Forty minutes later Cash for Cans coughed up a slip for one dollar eighty, redeemable at the checkstand, to cover about half the cost, I figured, of a six-pack of Chihuahua, Mexico's cheapest.

Inside Lucky, no deli, no espresso stand, only the jolt of refrigerated air, the heady familiar smell of cleanser and Pop Tarts.

The store was crowded. Sundresses and flip flops. Cutoff shorts. I was a minority, the white girl, shamefully aware of it after too long in the great white north. At the checkstand, the clerk studied me carefully, making me unreasonably nervous, certain that she was judging my expensive river sandals as if to say: Trader Joe's is across town.

"ID?" she monotoned.

I pulled out my driver's license.

"Washington," she said, changing her tone. "The state? Oh, I've heard it's beautiful. I want to move up there with my six-year-old."

No, no. I wanted to say. Stay put, can't we? California, for all its Scummymeads is as real, as authentic, as any place else.

"It rains a lot," I said.

"Oh," she said, retreating into surly silence.

"But you'd love it." I forced a smile, reined in hard on my Now Go Home attitude. "You ought to go," I said. "You really ought to go."

⟡

Late spring morning. The Jazz victorious again. I stand with my burlap sack ready to descend into the clear-cut again. Coming home, I think, is complicated. Susie writes sitcoms now, I hear. She's moved to Hollywood, people say, or to the beach. Mr. History is just that. My goddaughters are in high school, nearly out, not yet considering colleges near or far. They are submergers, homecoming princesses, and I am relieved for them. Wendell Berry, the literary conscience of those of us in river sandals, the last-best-place crowd, says to sink your roots and nurture them. And how we long to … if only we could figure out where. Easy enough, perhaps, if your family gives you a headstart, a hearty taproot several generations deep. Harder if your four grandparents left immigrant parents from four different nations in search of paradise—New York, Pennsylvania, Florida, Missouri, California—only to find it a moving target. I'm a California girl, sure, once and forever, but movement is my inheritance. Hope, my birthright. From above me, I can hear the guys debating basketball and the worth of their mutual funds. From below, I hear the river churning tumultuously, brimming with overripe snow, charging westward toward the Puget Sound, and farther along, to the Pacific. A light misty film coats my wool shirt as I work steadily, burning with a sometimes selfish passion for what I do, for where I live, brew pub or none. For now. I reach into my sack for the cuttings lopped from living willows last week, and I bend again, over and over, to tuck new trees-to-be into the muddy earth.

Children of the Woods

It's 7:15 a.m. and raining to beat hell as the four of us climb into the battered Forest Service Suburban. Jeremy, Dustin, and I have only been able to forestall departure by fifteen minutes, which means we have a particularly piss-poor mood to look forward to—Kevin, our foreman's. The rig reeks of saw gas and spilled pop cans of yesterday's tobacco spit—Jeremy and Dustin's. Kevin switches on the radio, spins the dial to NPR. Jeremy and Dustin shift in their seats, but remain silent. We have been through this before, and we have a strict radio truce: NPR in the morning, classic rock in the afternoon. The reception is sketchy. Something about Yasir Arafat.

"Yes, Sir, you are fat," Jeremy sniggers under his breath.

"Scattered showers near the mountains," the local news anchor predicts.

We all groan. That's us.

We pull in behind JV's Texaco Deli Mart at the only four-way intersection in Darrington, and because we have been warned repeatedly by our supervisors not to stop here during work hours (it does not look good to the locals, they argue), Kevin leaves the rig idling for a quick getaway. Kevin and I fill plastic thermamugs of coffee. Jeremy and Dustin buy an order of fried chicken gizzards and a Big Gulp each. Then, instead of returning to the Suburban lickety-split like he's supposed to, Kevin disappears. I figure he's at the pay phone, so I mill around a little longer and grab a couple of dusty bottles of three-dollar Andre champagne from behind the malt liquors.

"What's with him?" Dustin grumbles.

I shrug, not wanting to explain. Kevin has been trying for weeks to secure a ski-instructing job for the winter, and there have been a few offers, but he is choosy. Ruggedly handsome and maniacally fit, Kevin belongs in a Patagonia catalog. He belongs on the summit of a Himalayan peak, at the oars of a Colorado river raft, on the sheer face of Half Dome. This time of year, he belongs on skis, and he feels it. He's weary of the rain, of being the only one left in a bunkhouse built for twenty, of this late-season non-Wilderness trail work. Mostly he's sick of Jeremy and Dustin.

"Any luck?" I ask when Kevin returns.

"None," he says.

"Well, that sucks," Dustin offers.

Kevin steadies his foot on the accelerator.

After twenty more minutes of news from the Middle East, we turn off the gravel highway and lose radio reception. From here, the weavy logging road is badly washboarded from a fall of heavy use by deer hunters, so I crack a window to prevent myself from getting carsick. Jeremy zips his jacket to his throat. He shifts in his seat and begins to kick Dustin out of boredom. It's the usual routine. Jeremy is skinny, blond, and incurably hyperactive. When he is standing, he has the continuous distracting habit of hefting his crotch with one hand while he gestures with the other. Dustin is as strong as he is fat, as kind and imperturbable as he is lazy. He probably weighed 240 when he was sixteen, and he's well beyond that now at twenty-two; he takes up two-thirds of the backseat. Jeremy kicks. Dustin ignores him. As we approach the worksite, thirty-five miles out and three thousand feet above town, rain solidifies into thick silvery threads of sleet, and Dustin begins to snore.

In one seamless motion, Kevin cuts the motor and hops out. Before the rest of us have moved an inch, he's lugging a gas generator out onto the bridge. Jeremy and Dustin and I hover behind the Suburban, pulling on rain gear, slurping the last of our coffee, Mountain Dew, Dr. Pepper. We pick through the mangled jackstraw pile of tools—chainsaws and levels, axes and socket sets, a circular saw, electric drills—without enthusiasm.

Our fall project has been to replace a perfectly good drive-across bridge with a steel beam horse-and-hiker-only bridge. The road used to continue three miles beyond here and dead-end in a clear-cut, but logging completed (depleted, actually), the Forest Service has taken to rehabbing these old roads. So a Forest Service backhoe went up the road and tore out culverts and built up massive waterbars. Three weeks ago, the backhoe was the last vehicle to cross the drive-across bridge before a rented excavator yanked it out and put the I-beams for this one in place.

The four of us have been left with the plans and supplies to complete the project: cedar decking, handrails, lag screws, washers. We are unaccustomed to this sort of work. Normally we would be deeper in the woods on a real trail, not a road-turned-to-trail, and we would find our own materials, make our own design. Our egos are bruised here, and without a morning walk to temper our tempers, we are all running on short fuses.

But work is work. We asked for work, begged, actually, to stay on until Thanksgiving. Never mind the clouds, rain, sleet, spilled tobacco, blueprints from hell. I guess I ought to admit that Kevin is not the only one in a piss-poor mood.

⟨𝕒

When I lived in Darrington, several years ago now, I didn't know a single local except Jeremy and Dustin. I slept in the women's bunkhouse, a double-wide trailer partitioned with old office dividers, and littered with the junk of six of us who'd spend a week in the woods and then a couple of days driving "down below" to Everett or Seattle to go to movies and bookstores, to visit friends and family, to buy produce. Sometimes, when I couldn't face city traffic, or over time as the things that mattered to me migrated gradually closer, I shopped in Darrington, though the clerks at the IGA did not approve of my shopping habits. They would hold ginger root, say, or cilantro at arm's length. "What'd you say this was?" They'd frown on the grubby boyish fistfuls of cash I kept stuffed in my jeans pockets. They'd wait impatiently while I shoved thirty pounds of groceries into a daypack rather than use grocery sacks. I apologized awkwardly, or I took the paper bags without complaint. But if the clerks didn't say it, their scowls did: I didn't belong.

Jeremy and Dustin belonged. They were from Darrington most recently and originally from the bigger town, Arlington. "Drive north on I-5," Jeremy directed someone to his hometown, "'til you smell cowshit, then take a right." That would be Arlington: rivers braiding through farmland on the homestretch toward Puget Sound. Forty swervy miles farther the same direction, in dense timber beneath steep glaciated peaks, sits Darrington, a depressed logging town settled by former North Carolinians who were willing to risk life and limb cutting down gargantuan trees. Another Darrington boy, a coworker on a later crew, told me every man in his family had died either in a war or in a logging accident. Dustin's mother, probably hoping to cut her losses, picked up seasonal Forest Service jobs for Dustin and his best friend Jeremy when they were teenagers.

By the time I met them, Jeremy and Dustin were no longer teenagers. They were young men who loved to drink.

Once, another crew member, a ski instructor and a mountain-bike racer at thirty-five, tried to warn the boys.

"Man," he said, "I worry about your livers."

"Drinking's bad for your liver?" Jeremy asked.

"Yeah, it is." Eric said. Jeremy had boasted plenty of times that he'd drunk at least a six-pack a day since he was sixteen. If anything, we considered this a conservative estimate. "At the rate you're going, it'll be shot by the time you're thirty-five."

"Oh, if I got that long, then, no problem," Jeremy said with a grin.

With seven of us, the crew was large enough to break into two groups: one that backpacked miles into Glacier Peak Wilderness for regular trail maintenance and another that took on frontcountry construction projects—a new raft launch here, a wheelchair-accessible trail there. Backcountry projects offered spectacular scenery, solitude, enough physical activity to make you nauseous. Frontcountry projects offered every night at home, hot meals, hot showers, and close proximity to enough alcohol to make you really nauseous.

It wasn't that Jeremy and Dustin were incapable of doing backcountry work. If anyone on the crew could carry a heavy pack, it was Dustin. Since we had neither horses nor mules, he did it pretty often. On top of the inexplicable super-sized bags of corn chips and fist-sized alarm clocks Jeremy and Dustin each carried, Dustin would, with a little coaxing, shoulder a sledge hammer, a rock bar, a box of ten-inch spikes, some cable, a few explosives.

If anyone could use a crosscut saw, it was Jeremy. When a six-foot-diameter cedar fell across a major trail, suspended high above the tread (but still indisputably within the clearing limits for a horse trail), the rest of us lugged stepladders into the woods like loyal caddies. Jeremy carried the saw. The log had wedged itself so firmly between four or five standing trees that the resulting tension made it too dangerous for a second sawyer to perch on a ladder on the opposite side, so Jeremy single-bucked the whole thing. He gripped the saw handle in his right hand and cupped two fingers of his left hand between the sharp beveled teeth and the wide splayed rakers for control, then he sawed, smoothly, deftly, heaving his crotch each time he took a breather. He finished in just short of three hours. He'd been stoned the entire time.

At times, especially after work, Jeremy and Dustin seemed to enjoy the backcountry. They drank and smoked around the campfire with a tiny pair of Walkman speakers scratching out barely decipherable AC/DC or Black Sabbath. They cooked communal meals enthusiastically with quantity in mind: massive portions of dried Uncle Ben potatoes and gravy, multiple envelopes of Lipton instant soups. Out from under Kevin's watchful eye, they killed grouse with rocks in alpine meadows and roasted them for dinner.

"Children of the woods," they liked to holler for no reason. "We're children of the woods."

Even so, if they had a choice, as they did every Wednesday when the crew divided for the week, they'd stay in town.

Maybe I would've too, but since I had the least seniority, I had no choice. While Jeremy and Dustin and the boys drank, me and Kevin and Bridget ("the girls' crew," Jeremy and Dustin sniggered) marched. We covered more than a hundred miles each week, clearing blowdowns, repairing tread, brushing, brushing, brushing. I wore a Walkman for sanity. Between the headphones, I could lose myself in the rhythm, the repetition, and sink into a happily unthinking state, a Zen-like labor buzz, as I sawed and hacked through hemlock and silver fir, vine maple, slide alder, berry brambles, and ferns, then dug into the duffy mat of decomposing leaves, cones, needles, god knows what, three feet deep or six, I didn't care, working toward mineral soil to the sounds of the Dave Matthews Band or Nanci Griffith. Over time, I grew stronger and more skilled, more discerning, and I felt some satisfaction in the ache and sweat and, at the end of the day, the exhaustion.

Bridget and Kevin worked past quitting time as a rule. Ten hours of trail work was, for them, not enough. They prided themselves on miles walked, logs cut, shovelfuls of dirt moved. On their nights to prepare dinners, they presented lavish, extravagant meals: walnut and gorgonzola pizza, Thai roast beef salad. After dinner, they invited me to join them on extra off-trail hikes. Get a view, they'd say. Going to bed, I'd say. Have fun. There was something about their enthusiasm that felt, to me, half-greedy and half-guilty. I didn't want to earn the right to be in the woods by seeing as much as I could, or by proving how much extra work I could do, by carrying as much weight as I could, by cooking as elaborately as I could. I just wanted to be there. I wanted it to be that simple.

⟨ଈ

On the new bridge, sleet begins to gob into runny spurts of snow, coating the bridge, the rig, the tools, our rain gear. We work in pairs, and it's been the same pairs since early October when the rest of the crew was laid off: Jeremy and Dustin, me and Kevin. With Kevin, the name of the game is speed, and since I am still not as strong physically as he is, I earn my keep by staying one step ahead of him mentally.

"Do you have the three-eighths socket?"

"Right here."

"We're going to need more ..."

"Washers. Here."

I want to impress Kevin. I can't help it. He's that kind of guy. Besides at this point, there is tangible reward for working faster: we will be done. And I can hardly contain my excitement, though the truth is I have less of a winter plan than Kevin. I will be staying in a tiny cedar cabin north of town. Every now and then Kevin asks about what road trips I have planned, which ski areas I will hit. He acts jealous of my freedom in that sense, mostly because he is unfailingly polite. I don't dare tell him that after only five years of this seasonal life, half the number he's lived, I am starved for staying put.

While I ponder and drill and refill the chainsaw with gas, Kevin notices that Jeremy and Dustin have completed their handrail. As in completely done. Season over. They moved faster than we did, despite the fact that they are well aware that if we were to spend all day in the Suburban memorizing early-season NBA scores, we'd get paid the same, and more, we'd keep our jobs for another month, which wouldn't hurt them a bit. They've never been on skis. Not likely ever to be. In the off-season, they will collect unemployment and play in the weekly darts contest at the Red Top tavern for steaks—twenty frozen sirloins for the winner, ten for second place, five for third. Dustin will win a freezer full of steaks; he will gain weight. Jeremy will lose weight, growing evidence that alcohol is not his only drug of choice.

For now, Jeremy and Dustin perform a victory dance, sprinting toward each other, over and over, from either end of the bridge then skidding through the slop into a high five in the center. I go after the gas drill to finish the last three holes. Despite the heavy wet globs of snow, Kevin's taken off his gloves to ratchet even faster. I finish the drilling and stand back to watch this, the grand finale. One lag screw tight. Two. Jeremy and Dustin reload the Suburban with tools while Kevin ratchets for his life, red-eared. He is tightening the last one when, predictably, he drops the socket wrench into the creek below.

"I could put on the hip waders," I offer lamely, "and go after it."

Silence.

"Or we could drive back and get another one," Dustin says.

Finally, Kevin looks up at us and grins. "Forget it," he says. "Just forget it."

I have snapshots of that noon in a shoebox that I pull out every now and then. We are in plastic armor, muddy green and yellow rain suits, ill-fitting hard hats. In one, Kevin is waving the bottle of champagne in the air. There are a couple obligatory shots of Jeremy and Dustin showering each other World Series style, and there is one of Jeremy and Dustin each holding one of my feet on their knees like a cheerleaders' pyramid, the three of us framed by a cedar handrail. There's a hint of yearbook drama in it all. Friends forever. Have a happy winter. We're outta here! But it's genuine enough. For once it didn't matter where we were from or where we were going, only that we'd finished the bridge, that we'd survived, that the snowy season had arrived in earnest, and who wouldn't be excited, skier or not, by the change? No longer the interminably drawn-out ending, but now a beginning. The pictures are blurred by the slush, and my memories, too, of that day and the rest, have blurred and reshaped themselves into tall tales in which Jeremy and Dustin star as goofy superheroes. What my stories neglect to mention, as I repeat them regularly, is that I always envied them, their ease and their exuberance—their unquestioned sense of belonging—and that, perhaps absurdly, I feel I owe them a debt.

⌘

I thought about that debt a lot, even back then. I tried to make sense of a gnawing sense of cultural unease, one I could not precisely define, but which, in my memory, attaches itself to one day when I picked up a hitchhiker in a rainstorm.

Up the road from the Darrington Ranger Station, at the confluence of the Suiattle and Sauk rivers, sat another government compound, cleared entirely of trees and speckled with boxy paint-faded houses in surreal arrangement: within spitting distance of the rivers, the houses faced inward, toward each other, cul-de-sac style. I had never stopped there because I never had reason to until I saw the wet stranger, thumb out, and I pulled over.

The hitchhiker was silent and more than a little menacing. When I asked where he was headed, he turned away from me to display streams of blood pouring from a gash above his left eye. He cradled a soaked cotton sweatshirt on his lap, in which I decided—not too unreasonably from the sense of things—he may have been hiding a weapon. Eventually he announced: "Here," right beside the strange compound and its small sign: "Sauk/Suiattle Indian Reservation." That Native Americans lived in Darrington did not surprise me. That they lived poorly did not surprise me either, though it's hard to look that fact in the bleeding face without feeling deep nauseating grief for the past and an urgent need to overlook (to ignore? to forget? to forgive?) the gun-in-his-lap details of the present. He got out and slammed the door.

The timber industry was flailing, booming and busting in the post-Spotted Owl shakedown. Bedroom communities were seeping upriver unseen. Change was encroaching, and it felt to me a little like those of us working seasonally for the Forest Service might be the first wave. We didn't really need to assimilate since we could live safely, insularly, on a compound. We could drive down below for culture. We could behave any way we pleased because, ugly truth be told, over time, in terms of benefits received from listening hours, NPR would win hands down over twenty-five-year-old glam rock, and probably, unless nutritionists took another one-eighty, whole grains would outlive fried chicken gizzards. Over there in the mossy loamy woods, in that landscape overblessed with water where for a time I felt more content than anywhere I'd ever lived, it was that complex labeled sadness—who displaces who—that set my mind spinning.

It's easy, a hundred years after chasing them off, to sympathize with Native Americans. We were terribly wrong, and try as we might we can't think of a thing to do to make it right. In the bargain, perhaps rightly, Native Americans get rewritten as heroes. Even though it's hard to imagine red-suspendered loggers ever redrawn in saintly garb, I never could shake my discomfort about displacing them. After all, loggers didn't decide to decimate the forests. We bought the lumber, all of us, we buy it still, and we buy stock in the international corporations that run the whole beastly show, and even if those arguments are old as the hills, even if it's apples and oranges—the Indians were here for thousands of years; the Tarheels only a couple hundred—I'm still bothered. I'm not making a moral argument. I'm not saying that it's wrong, in general, for city folks to drive property taxes out of reach of working folks or even, say, to take their jobs on trail crews. I'm just saying that, in the particular, it was awfully sad.

On the ride home, I stare out the window happily buzzed. The radio is louder than usual. Kevin is driving fast. Def Leppard. Van Halen. Fishtailing over the slip-and-slide washboard. Jeremy playing air guitar in his lap. Dustin snoring again. Past clear-cuts piled with sopping slash. Past a small hand-carved sign: "Big Cedar" with an arrow. Which one? There is only one left? Onto the gravel highway, snow giving way to rain as we descend through thicker, tighter doghair forests, second growth, then third, then alder, alder, alder. Beer cans—Schmidt's always Schmidt's—lining the ditch. Over a snow-swollen creek, salmon the size of my leg fighting their way upstream, undulating in the froth like so many flexing fingers. As we hit the pavement, twenty minutes to go, "Bohemian Rhapsody" comes on the radio. Jeremy and Dustin know these lyrics, though the song is older than they are, from *Wayne's World* in which they failed to recognize Wayne and Garth as fairly accurate caricatures of themselves. Dustin unslouches to join Jeremy in a full-volume sing-along.

I laugh. I know the lyrics, too, and I'm dying to sing along. I've been on the girls' crew all summer, with oversized calves and a somewhat healthier liver to prove it, and I've sided firmly with NPR all fall, but I've damned well had it.

Wet pavement splatters from the front tires obscure my back-window view of mildewed double-wides, shiny new American trucks parked out front, bumperstickers reading, "Hug a logger. You'll never go back to trees," snarling dogs testing the limits of their chains. I want to sing, but decide against it, and I'm glad. Jeremy and Dustin have rehearsed their parts, and they put on an impressive show, alternating between soaring falsettos and deep croaky pretend baritones.

I applaud when they finish. Kevin seethes silently instead. He is not about to encourage Jeremy and Dustin one iota more. He's tired and frustrated, single-minded, headed down the road back to the bunkhouse, and in a week or less, to the ski area and the better life. Eventually, in not too many years, Kevin will move on to become a telemark ski guide out of Aspen and a trail crew leader in Glacier National Park, just as Bridget and I will be promoted to permanent status as leaders of our own respective crews. Trails wind and switchback, seasons pile one upon the next, and though we were never children of the woods—suburban refugees all three of us—when we crouch in yet another autumn rainstorm making shavings with a pocketknife to start the evening fire, we will have become, well, grownups of the woods.

Jeremy and Dustin, it turns out, are headed down a different road. The muddied details filtered in over the course of the winter ahead. Jeremy stole Dustin's paycheck and forged Dustin's signature, a federal crime. Then Jeremy claimed that Dustin had either (a) told him he could or (b) owed him the money anyway. Neither alibi looked likely to shelter Jeremy from federal criminal proceedings until, eventually, Dustin refused to participate. Jeremy avoided jail time and only lost his job on trail crew. He foundered away from the woods, apparently: worked construction, collected unemployment, worked construction again, got drunk, got high. It's all hearsay and myth now since I never saw him again, and it's not a story I like to repeat because it's not mine and, mostly, because what starts out all Wayne and Garth and goofy cartoonish fun ends all wrong.

It was winter, the season of drizzle and nothing-to-do, when Jeremy and Dustin drove up a logging road and passed a Jeep stuck in the mud. As is backroads protocol, Jeremy and Dustin hooked a chain to the Jeep and hauled the folks, a young couple, out. Thanks and see ya. On their way back down, they passed the couple again. Stuck again. Pulled them out a second time. No problem. Here the story breaks down logistically. Whichever way they were driving, Jeremy and Dustin somehow passed the couple a third time, stuck a third time, and this time refused to help. The stuck guy got a little panicky, a little embarrassed, maybe, in front of his girlfriend, and eventually, very, very angry. I can picture how it happened: Jeremy heaving his crotch, picking his forehead, throwing his head back and laughing too loudly. The guy pulled a gun. Then Jeremy, whose coordination, as I recall, always peaked with inebriation, pulled a baseball bat. It could not have been pretty.

That's the last I ever heard of Jeremy. Dustin lost his trails job shortly thereafter. He hung on with the Forest Service as a firefighter until just before his thirtieth birthday, when he could no longer pass the fitness test required. The failure, his supervisor explained to me with a shrug, had been a long time coming.

☞

After we've parked the Suburban on the compound and wrestled the tools from the back end, dried them with rags, drained their gas, and locked them up until spring, I say my goodbyes, hugging a little long, but refusing the invitation to the Red Top all the same. I will have left Darrington by the next year, as it turns out, moved on to a job on the sunnier eastside of the Cascades in a national park where crews are more blandly homogenous: university-bred and often vegetarian. Before I leave in the early spring I will return to tighten the final lag screw on the new bridge, still unused at that point, because of the time of year, yes, but also because it is too in-between: the roads too rough for horse trailers to navigate, the trail too road-like for backpackers who seek true wilderness, places untrodden. By summer, I know, fireweed and ferns will shoot upwards in the unobstructed sun, then over time, alder, then maple, fir, hemlock, even cedar eventually, and hikers will arrive content, unable to detect the scars. Succession happens.

Meanwhile I head north on the highway, driving too fast because I am so happy to be finished. When I cross the bridge over the Sauk River, I watch a bald eagle below flapping its wings with a salmon captured in its talons, still fighting, and I am so excited to have seen such a thing that I drive even faster. I squeal around one corner, then the next, and I turn up the radio to sing along to any song I please, any song at all. I am thinking about changes, the ones behind me, the ones to come, and how easy they can be: natural and inevitable, shocking and horrifying as the deer that launches like a cliché into the highway in front of me not five miles from my cedar cabin. I race around a blind curve and hit the deer, just barely, the side of the station wagon glancing the side of the animal, injuring it perhaps, before I even know what's happened. I pull over to see what harm I've done, to see what, if anything, I might do to make it right. I search awhile in the darkening woods, then give up and continue towards home.

How to Waste Time

We were repairing the handrail on a footlog, a sturdy footlog, one that maybe didn't need a handrail, but one that had always had one. The handrail had offered hikers an added measure of security. Our problem was simple. We could take the handrail off, ten minutes with the chainsaw, or repair the bent-over post, a two-hour test of patience. We gazed down into the frothy early-season snowmelt rushing beneath us and chose the latter. We tromped into the woods, picked out a saucer-sized diameter Alaskan cedar that had fallen sometime in the winter, and were in the process of pasting it in when a backpacker approached.

The backpacker was talkative, and his accent was Bostonian, I think. In the telling of the story it's been exaggerated to where all his r's are w's. But it was less dramatic than that, something understated, if still a little out of place. He was in his early sixties, probably, with the kind of gray beard and ragged look that I associate with the pre-hippies that must've hung around with my dad in San Francisco in the 1950s. He'd clearly hiked before, was no newcomer, no wannabe, just a lonely man from Boston or San Francisco who went to the trouble of finding his way to these mountains, instead of any others, to spend a couple of weeks walking. Maybe because he only had a couple weeks, he had a guidebook that he described to us. The book, through clever marketing, was called *How Not to Waste Time in the North Cascades*. The idea, like the idea of many hiking guides, was to define what was and what was not worth seeing. Spare the hiker with precious little vacation time from, well, wasting time. The backpacker watched us work on the handrail for a while, then asked where we were headed the next day.

"Bridge Creek," I answered.

"Bridge Creek," he said, remembering the description from his guidebook. "Pretty boring, huh?"

The backpacker waited for an answer, but I could not think of one. We spend the equivalent of three or four weeks each summer walking and working on Bridge Creek trail. From snow to mud to dust and back to snow again. And the truth, though I hate to admit it, is that Bridge Creek is sort of boring. It meanders up the drainage at a steady grade through rocky gorges and thick brush. Views are only intermittent. The sound of running water. Blah Blah Blah. Anyone who has hiked anywhere has been on a trail like Bridge Creek. It's one of those stretches of the Pacific Crest Trail, the two-thousand-plus mile connect-the-dot trail from Canada to Mexico, that makes some hikers call it the Pacific Valley Trail, a place where surveyors kept the trail low to defray costs of construction and maintenance and to protect the high alpine meadows. Still, when the backpacker who pronounced "boring" like "Boeing" criticized Bridge Creek, I felt a little defensive.

"It's all right," my new boss, Phil, philosophized after the hiker had moved on down the trail, while I held the new post upright with all my body weight waiting for it to be spiked into place. "The way some people see it, stuff like this is a waste of time."

He held the sledge and hammered gently, patiently, against the spike until the handrail stood upright again. It might last one season, I thought, or it might last ten.

"The way I see it," he said, "most of life is a waste of time anyway, so why worry about it?"

But I did worry. It's not a matter of wasting time, I thought, but a matter of what we notice. Sometimes, for example, I forget to notice wildflowers. I take in stride the brilliant red yellow columbine, the fleshy pink Indian paintbrush, tiger lilies drooping from the stalks, trillium, chocolate lilies, twin flowers, bleeding hearts. Sometimes they're at ankle level so I accidentally step on them. Sometimes they're lost among the encroaching berry brambles and devils club that I take down in one swipe of a brush whip. When I do notice the flowers, what else am I missing? Should I define the trail by the flowers? Or by the red huckleberry meadows of fall, bears teaching their cubs to collect berries in one swipe of a paw? By the snowy corniced ridges of spring or by the gray stark granite of late summer? Complete this sentence: these mountains are … . That sentence would take too much time.

⟜

A little later in the summer, I picked up a couple of hitchhikers after work, a young peachy-bearded man with oversized quads and his even younger girlfriend. Turns out the guy was writing a book about the trails in the area, so I mentioned the *Waste of Time* book. He groaned. His book, he explained, was nothing like that.

"I'm a biologist," he said. "I'm focusing on flora and fauna."

He listed for me, as we drove up the road, the Latin name for every plant in the valley. And beneath my irritation, I was jealous. He had somehow learned, through books and a short time visiting, things I didn't know or hadn't noticed while I was wasting time with novels and handrails. I listened to his litany while I fiddled with the choke on the truck. I learned a lot.

I offered the hitchhikers a cold drink at the cabin, but the guy declined. He told his girlfriend to hang out for a bit, then head to camp to fix supper. He had one more trail to cover before nightfall, so I was left alone with the young woman. She was eager to talk, and bragged liberally about the boyfriend who had already written guides about three other mountain ranges, one per summer. Usually he camped the whole summer, covered as many trails as he could. I asked if she'd been along the year before. No, she said, there had been another girl. She had met him in the spring at the counter of the diner she worked in. She had followed him, never having backpacked before, and was now in charge of meals and other unnamed duties. I wondered if she had wearied yet of the situation, when she would, or if that is how the summer was planned: for her to weary of him at just the right moment, the end of the season, when he could retreat to a friend's living room to write his biology.

"He went to college," she boasted, "for almost two years."

I nodded. I spent six years in college and still can't justify reducing the mountains to my own limited perspective. Cowardliness, I know. I just don't believe I've been here long enough to say.

The sun slipped behind the ridge top and the evening breeze turned cool.

"I have to go inside," I apologized. Dinner to make. Lunch to pack. Novels to read. Sleep to get. Time is everything.

⇥

After that, I thought maybe the problem is not what we notice, or don't notice. It's what we expect. We want things to be as we imagine them, and at some point they are not. The trail is not postcard perfect. The handrail buckles under the snow load. The boyfriend is a scumbag. Well, how do you plan for this? All that time and energy wasted in anticipation. Then the punchline doesn't make sense.

⇥

Once, a few years ago, I spent the summer solstice working a trail along a high ridge, one of the finest places I know. But my crewmate Jeremy, a native of the dark lush westside Cascades, felt uncomfortable in that high country. During the 10:00 p.m. solstice sunset, with soft rolling snow-and-flowers meadows spotlit and shadowy in the last of the light, the rest of the crew walked a half mile behind Jeremy and me, pointing out peaks in the distance, naming glaciers, pretending to see the Puget Sound.

"Look at that," Jeremy said, turning back to see what was taking them so long. "They dig this shit." Utter disgust.

Later, in the historic fire lookout where we spent the night, Jeremy pulled out his Walkman and speakers to play AC/DC's *Back in Black*, the heavy metal classic, while the northern lights reflected snowy ridges of the dormant volcano across the way. The rest of the crew feigned sleep in frustration. Wrong soundtrack. Jeremy and I stayed awake drinking cheap whiskey from a white gas container labeled "Not Fuel."

I asked him, "Why *Back in Black*?"

"Well, I asked myself," he explained, "what's the only album that everybody loves?"

"*Back in Black*?" I guessed.

"Right on," he said. He leaned his head back on his sleeping bag to take in the guitar solo on "Highway to Hell." When it ended, he turned to me.

"Tomorrow, right?" he said. "Tomorrow we get to go back down."

It occurred to me then, though I often forget, that magic, like music, can be a matter of personal preference.

ᘒ

I finally found the book not long ago. *How Not to Waste Time.* It was pretty catchy, really. There was a boot print system. One boot for a lousy trail. Four for an extra special good one. A boot with a circle and a slash through it meaning: Don't Go There. I thought I could label my trail days the same way. Even when they're all on the same trail. One day is a four boot. One's a boot with a slash through it. Might be the wildflowers or the company, the sunset or the soundtrack, the weather, the bugs, fitness or diet or the stage of the moon. Might be what I notice, or what I expect. Might be me. There's no saying for sure. Seems now like a waste of time to try to figure it out.

The Tourists in My Yard

Ten o'clock in the morning, and I am still lying in bed when a renovated school bus, sky blue with a painted rainbow on either side, pulls up behind my rusted Dodge pickup. About fifteen tourists disembark and fan out through the pines to look down off a high bridge to the place, just outside my bedroom window. No outside roads access this remote valley, which is separated from the rest of the world by a fifty-five-mile-long fjord-like lake flanked on either side by huge expanses of Wilderness. The bus and the pickup arrived some years back on a barge that runs once a month or so. The tourists arrived on a passenger boat that runs once a day. Now they are watching a mountain river charge through a narrow rocky gorge eighty feet deep. I know this number, eighty, not because I've ever bothered to tote a tape measure out through the kinnikinnick for verification. I know it because I hear the Park Service concessionaire announce it regularly when I ride the boat out, as I do every few weeks, to get groceries or to use a telephone.

"Sign up for the grand tour," the amplified voice, sugary sweet and overly loud, invites, "to High Bridge, the site of an historic ranger station in a spectacular setting beside an eighty foot gorge."

"At High Bridge, you will see all varieties of wildlife," the voice promises. "Mule deer. Black bear. Maybe even a cougar."

It's raining this morning, a colder rain for July than the summer-clothed tourists expected. It's colder, I admit, than I expected. I shivered as I half-jogged to the outhouse in my T-shirt. I suspect that any deer or bear are hiding, either from the rain or, more likely, from the growl of the idling bus. Where the cougars are I couldn't say, since in several summers working in these mountains, I have never seen one. I am a little suspicious of the tour boat's truth-in-advertising.

As the tourists file back from the overlook, they peek into the cabin windows curiously, a little guiltily, like gawkers at a car wreck. I understand the attraction. The cabin, painted dull government green over cedar shingles, looks exactly like the sort of museum where an amateur actor might be dressed in costume for a living history demonstration. Only difference is, there's an official-looking, computer-generated large-font sign right beside the door that reads: Private Residence—Emergency Inquiries Only. I am relieved to see most of the tourists notice the sign, fill their plates at the rustic log table where the driver has set out a lunch of fried chicken and potato salad, and clamber back onto the bus where the heater still runs.

The grand tour costs twenty dollars. The folks out there paid twenty bucks to eat lukewarm food while sitting on a school bus. I should feel sorry for them. They spent four hours on a boat, then another hour on a bus, to eat a lousy twenty-dollar lunch where I pay thirty dollars a month rent to live. I should feel lucky, spoiled even, I know. But I can't help it. I wish they would go home.

༒

Today is my first day off in eight. I've been out camping and clearing brush from along the Pacific Crest Trail, swinging a weed whip, the modern safety version of a scythe, through the ferns and berry brambles that obscure the trail within weeks after snowmelt if we don't follow behind cutting an eight-foot-wide swath. My hands this morning, as a result, are gnarled blocks, stuck semi-permanently in the shape of a weed whip handle. I can open the fingers of one hand with the backside of the other only for the sake of coffee. And this is precisely what I'm doing, pawing open a paper filter, when a straggler pounds on the loose screen door.

"Is there a ranger here?" a middle-aged man asks politely.

"No, I'm sorry," I say. "Can I help you?"

It's true I'm not a ranger. I'm a laborer. The distinction in the Park Service is clear. Even the hats are stratified—Smokey Bear Stetsons for rangers, foam ball caps for laborers—and I am not complaining. I like the shovel-and-pulaski simplicity of my trail crew job: no computers, no phone, no meetings, just gnarled fingers clamped around a coffee mug.

"Well, do you have any brochures?"

The stranger cranes his neck to peer into the front room at the work boots steaming by the woodstove, muddy rain gear hanging from hooks in the ceiling, *National Geographic* maps of the former Soviet republics pinned to grimy walls. The cheapest wallpaper. He lifts one eyebrow, expecting perhaps that I will be disarmed by his gracious manner.

"No," I tell him, frustration mounting, "I live here. Is this an emergency?"

"Oh no, no, nothing like that."

I watch him shrug sheepishly, scuff one shiny new leather boot against another absently. He realizes his mistake, I think, and he is probably more lonely than curious. I consider, briefly, inviting him in for coffee. Surely, that is how I would wish to be treated if I were in his awkward new boots. But I have no energy for it. If today is typical, he'll be just the first of maybe a dozen people—folks who apparently turn functionally illiterate on vacation—to knock on that screen door. I am tired. I want so badly to drink my coffee, read my novel, lie still by the fire. Sleep, maybe. Alone.

"I'm sorry," I tell him none too graciously, "I live here."

I close the door, then watch out the bedroom window as he wanders, fists in his pockets, toward the bridge to gaze down at the river. And I worry about what's become of me in a decade of half-a-year laboring: I'm beginning to have sympathy for the Sagebrush Rebels.

In the late 1980s, I watched with horror a makeshift parade in the nearest town to my first seasonal job. Bulldozers draped in American flags crept down wide manicured streets, followed by cheering Boy Scouts and very large road-worn American pickups. It was an anniversary celebration of sorts, a victory dance of sorts for the day in 1979 when bulldozers plowed a trough into a nearby roadless area, Wilderness-to-be.

I stood a short distance apart from the parade, imagining machines chomping through junipers and pinyons, and I could feel the passion in the air: equal parts hatred and devotion, certainly capable of violence. I was scared. And I was wise enough, me in my sandals—the regulation footwear of a "flower sniffer"—to climb back in my Toyota and drive away.

Driving back toward my temporary mobile trailer home, where I could read Ed Abbey and write poetry in relative peace, I goaded myself into a moral tizzy. So this, I thought, was the Sagebrush Rebellion I had read about in *High Country News*, in *Sierra*. These local folks, miners mostly, and others throughout the small-town West, so I had read, were waging small-scale war against the feds for cramping their extractive-industry lifestyles with environmental regulations. I was fresh from the university and well-versed in theories about the historical roots of Western land conflicts. The paraders were victims of colonization, I told myself, duped by big-business interests, by distant land barons who would rape the land again and again. The theories suggested that their passion that summer day was born of economic necessity and ignorance.

Looking out my window today, unreasonably furious with the strangers out there, I am less sure. Those theories were, I think, devised in an office. The Sagebrushers' outrage must have been more personal than the loss-of-jobs rhetoric allows. They had worked that pristine canyon, the one the government had decided to preserve for those of us in search of the Nature Grail. They had hacked at the rocks, trailed after underfed cattle, shoveled, chipped, sweat, cursed, and learned, over time, how to do it—whatever it might be—right. Their parade was the plainest sort of Take-Back-What's-Mine.

ⒸⳐ

My crew, four of us, camped last week four thousand feet above the valley floor in a dark mixed-conifer forest—lodgepole, cedar, fir. The clouds settled in and began to spittle on Day One. We had to use a liter of chainsaw gas to start the campfire. By morning, the spittle had become steady rain. We smacked weed whips against the sopping stalks of willow and ash, huckleberry and fern. For most of the afternoon, I worked alone on a stretch of trail, itself no more than a gully of washed-over rocks, beside a slow meandering creek. I slipped occasionally off the edge of mossy banks and soaked my boots. When the day warmed up, black flies descended and clung to my clothes, trying to bite through layers of soggy wool. I'd sweep the palm of my work glove across my face and roll a dozen flies between my fingers, popping them apart like so many pimples.

It's not hard to imagine what I fantasized about: a warm dry office, a computer screen, a padded swivel chair. I've had opportunities to do that kind of work, and so far I've always turned them down. But out there in the brush it sounded pretty good. After all, I could visit national parks on sunny days, on bugless days, hike above tree line, carry no tools.

I stilled myself for a moment. I sopped the sweat from my eyebrows, pulled the Walkman headphones from my ears, and listened to the familiar rumble of water rushing down the impossibly steep mountainsides through brush fields and narrow gorges to the Columbia, to the Pacific. When I returned to brushing, swinging upwards, boxwood tumbling into the trail by the armload, I traced the paths of water back through my memory, back through high open meadows to craggy not-too-distant peaks, icy and ominous. They were paths I had followed before, and would likely follow again, on foot and in imagination. The office fantasy dulled in comparison.

A marmot lived in the toilet hole at our camp. She had a great life. Plenty of nourishment, apparently, and a great view to boot: the view from the shitter in the early morning, 5:30 when the sky is neither gray nor blue, was of nearby glaciers illuminated pink and orange. During the day, while we were out working, the marmot wreaked havoc in camp, chewing pack straps and knocking over tent poles, the marmot version of Take-Back-What's-Mine. She chomped through my toothpaste tube in the time it took me to turn and spit. It's a shame, I know, when marmots, like small-town Westerners and half-a-year laborers, become unnaturally dependent on outside sources of wealth and security, but I'm telling you: this marmot had it good.

There is another knock on the screen.

"Can you fill this?" A young woman in a tie-dye T-shirt and bike shorts cradles an empty plastic Nalgene water bottle in her hand. She looks my age, thirtyish, and I wonder, because of the tie-dye, if she might have attended the same university I did. I think to ask, but decide against it. The young woman is impatient and irritable. More likely she is dehydrated. The grand tour rarely includes enough drinking water.

"I'm sorry," I explain, more graciously now that I've had my coffee, "we have no running water here. No electricity."

The woman stands her ground, thinking perhaps that I am lying, or bragging, or complaining, none of which escapes her judgment.

"Do you live here?"

"Yes, for half the year. I work on the trail crew."

"Oh," she says, changing her tone. "That must be fun."

I stretch the fingers of my blocky fists instinctively, trying against resistance to open them back up.

"Yeah," I say, smiling, "it is. It's hard work, you know, but …"

"Where do you get your water?" she interrupts.

"From the river," I say, realizing I had misread her change of tone and feeling vaguely tricked. I direct her toward the steep trail down into the gorge. This is partially true. Sometimes I drink river water. Usually I haul four-gallon buckets up the dirt road from the shop in the Dodge. I have a mostly empty bucket in the back room now, and I feel like the surly clerk at the Texaco, pretending to have no bathroom.

"Oh, is that safe?" she asks.

I run through the script in my mind, trying to find the easy answer. It's a very clean river, I could tell her. The ever-churning trip through the gorge aerates the water more thoroughly than any purification plant. Giardia is a minor threat, yes, probably from backpackers upstream. Then again, it's pretty early in the season for backpackers.

"Are you sure it's safe?" she asks again. "I'm a nurse."

"If you're thirsty enough," I say finally, and I close the door.

She stands for a moment, confused, and more irritated now than when she first knocked. Then she turns and heads for the trailhead, apparently here to stay for the afternoon, to take a hike and enjoy the scenery.

I lie back down with my coffee, but I have no interest in reading. I stare instead at the crisscross pattern raindrops trace along a crack in the window.

I worked for a short while as an interpreter, one of the rangers in straw Stetsons who give nature walks and campfire talks and who, in large part, give the Park Service its loyal constituency. I was paid to learn about the place I just arrived in and recount it to visitors eager for a young and earnest uniformed voice. A fine job, a noble job, but it left me with the same discomfort that I felt the summer I worked for a nonprofit group in Mexico setting up community gardens: "Here I am knowing nothing and telling you about it."

It's easier just to work. Work in the woods can be too easily romanticized, exaggerated like a mighty fish story (I carry an eighty pound pack every day, really, more like ninety), but it is, at least, more about learning than knowing. It's taken me an awfully long time to learn a very little bit: which way to swing, for one; which plants yield to the weed whip, which require a saw; on which trails to carry extra water, on which to carry extra clothes; where to carry a rock pick, where an ax; when I'm just regular tired and when I am so tired that I can't go on.

I remember as a kid considering the irony that people who kill things know them best: hunters know animals, loggers know trees. I had it all wrong. It's not the killing. It's the work. Tree planters also know trees; packers know mules; trail workers, sometimes, know trails. At first it confused me, how rarely a skilled laborer will explain a thing. It's beginning to make sense.

❧

A little boy on a rented mountain bike three sizes too big is popping wheelies off-trail, tearing through the mud and through the long brittle fingers of kinnikinnick. I'm fantasizing now, as I often do, about the Homestead Act. As if I could, here in the twenty-first century be the first to settle this place overlooking the river where archaeologists have found evidence of settlements dating back thousands of years. As if, because I have left the ligament of my right knee, some function of my right shoulder, and all of my twenties on the trails through these woods, as if that makes this place mine. It does, doesn't it?

Well, frankly, no. I learned my poor manners from examples like Ed Abbey who, like me, fled the city for a subsidized paradise, then whined about letting anyone else in. I know that the tourists in my yard own this park as much as I do. More probably, as Abbey would say, because their salaries almost certainly pump more taxes into the federal government than mine do. But sometimes the way they behave—the way we behave, I should say, since I frequent public lands in the off-season and I know that I behave precisely the same way—disturbs me more than a bulldozer through prospective wilderness.

We parade into a new place like a new condo, expecting it to be comfortable and ready to be used according to our own whims. And we are particularly bad in national parks, where the relative ease of access, along with stringently enforced rules, reinforces our false sense of comfort. No, here I will not go on an Abbeyesque tirade against industrial tourism. I'll leave the poor RV folks out of the tussle since they can't even reach the district where I work. I will say this, though: flower sniffers can be as ugly as the rest. We take the intellectual high ground and act as if we already know the lay of the land because we have read the right books, gone to the right universities, been paid, perhaps, to live in our own private paradises. It serves me right when, after an exhausting day of trail work, I face the hiker who wants to give me an impromptu naturalist talk on the black bears in the area. ("No," he insists, "I'm sure it was a grizzly.") If we are the folks trying to protect public lands, no wonder Sagebrush Rebels get up in arms.

↙

It's 12:30 p.m., nearly time for the chicken lunchers to leave, and I am growing impatient, checking the window more often. I gaze out to see two women huddled together on soggy cottonwood rounds that my crew cut earlier in the season to serve as rustic seats for the customers on the grand tour. The women are eating their fried chicken outside, having refused, apparently, to get back on the bus. They look underdressed, and they look, actually, to be enjoying themselves. One, a small Asian woman, holds a bare hand out from beneath the drippy fir limbs. She holds it cupped, ignoring her lunch, and I cannot imagine what she is doing. I watch for a while, intrigued, until eventually I realize: she is catching raindrops. She laughs with her head laid back against her shoulders as she shakes the cold water out. Then she pulls her hand in, shivering dramatically, and shoves it into the pocket of her thin windbreaker. The colorful lightweight scarf draped over her head has shifted, in the process, to nearly cover her eyes. The other woman, who looks remarkably like my mother, gleefully tosses bread crumbs to an overfed gray squirrel. When she hears the bus driver lie on the horn, she dumps the remains of her overpriced lunch onto the ground, then reaches across the re-tie the scarf under her companion's chin. They walk slowly together back to the bus, stopping for a moment to look over, one last time, into the spectacular eighty-foot gorge.

🐇

The marmot and me and Ed Abbey and the Sagebrush Rebels, we all want the same thing: we want our place to ourselves. And I don't know how to escape this. It seems too much like free love, this idea that we can share land, that a place as intimate as my lover can belong to whoever pays twenty dollars for fried chicken and potato salad. I've courted the idea of being an interpreter again, of teaching people how to behave as the only means of protecting the place. But I rebel. I'm ashamed of it, truly, my selfishness, but the sad truth is that I don't want to show people how to behave. I would never show a stranger how to please my lover. Or, I should say, if I did, we could never have the same relationship. I would have to leave.

🐇

Sometimes I'm afraid that's how this story ends, the way it does every fall, with my work clothes in a dumpster, and thinking this: you can only share the place you love for so long before you want to call in the bulldozers. And maybe, with that in mind, leaving is not such a bad idea. Even Ed Abbey moved to Tucson, bought land, settled for long vacations and imaginary rebellions. But I am young still and more idealistic than I like to admit. I aspire to a selflessness that can overcome my uncertainties. That is, in fact, how I want this story to end:

❧

What ties us to the ground we walk on is not poetry or admiration or education. It's time and work and love. There are plenty of reasons to hope that wherever the tourists in my yard live and work, they love that place with a vicious, proud love. But what ties us to each other is the unspoken generosity that allows us to let others live and learn.

There's a knock on the door, and I answer.

"Do you have any water?"

I turn away from the open door, leaving the woman on the front step to wonder. I walk out the back door, grab an empty bucket, and stumble, tennis shoes sliding over loose dirt, down three steep switchbacks into the gorge. I squat for a moment on the bank watching water tumble and rage. I remove the lid and set the bucket in the current, bracing with all my weight against my own imbalance and against the force of the river. I pull the bucket out and slog back up the trail, dragging the bucket behind me.

The woman sits on my porch, watching pine needles rise slowly to the surface of muddy puddles. She hesitates when she sees me approach, then she holds out her empty quart bottle. I heave the four gallons to my waist, and I pour.

Long Distance

We wanted to run. That's why we'd come. We had our sneakers and our N.F.L. striped kneesocks, all of us kids he'd recruited himself from different elementary schools. But Coach Halpin would have none of it. He lined us up by height along the bike racks, and since I was the smallest, I was closest to him.

"Lean forward," he said and lunged with his front leg bent and his back leg straight. "Stretch your calf."

I didn't know that word yet. I pictured a baby cow. I mimicked Coach Halpin's pose, leaning forward so the top of the bike rack tucked under my chin guillotine-style, and I studied the man beside me. Though his legs were skinny and sprouted grey whiskery hairs, his muscles—quads, hamstrings, calves, so many new words— roped one around the other, trimly, and bulged in places I never expected. I admired his legs, and thought, since he was so danged serious about it, that stretching must have been how they got that way. I aspired to it. I lunged forward, eyes scrunched tight in concentration, wishing with all my might for great stony knobs to appear behind my shins.

"That's good," Coach Halpin said.

He was chewing gum, this muscled man, and he smiled at me, and I was in love like only an eight-year-old girl can be.

"You were made for distance," Coach said a couple weeks later. "You're a natural."

I knew what he really meant: that I was not fast, but I followed directions well. At practice each day we stretched then took a long slow lap around Hunt's Park: the ball fields, the swimming pool drained for winter, the playground with the spaceship monkey bars.

I heeled at Coach's side, always, while the other kids raced ahead full-bore like labs off leash, like I would have wanted to if I hadn't been so busy staring at Coach.

"You'll be a miler," he said.

"O.K.," I said.

Coach wore a nylon U.C.L.A. tank that showed off his arms—biceps, triceps!—and a Marine Corps tattoo. My dad had been a Marine so I recognized the logo, but my dad didn't have the tattoo, or the muscles. He'd played football in college, but now he usually lay on the couch with a beer watching television. We watched the Montreal Olympics together, Dad and I, and I did the math. I would achieve greatness in Moscow when I would be twelve, then repeat the feat in '84 when I'd be sixteen, then I'd retire.

I attended practice regularly, fanatically, even when practice moved from Hunt's Park out to the fringes of town where instead of lawn and sidewalk we ran on hard-packed dirt. We followed fire roads along irrigation canals into orange groves and up desert foothills where deep eroded ruts snaked toward me threatening to snap my ankles as I strained for the crest on my tiptoes. I felt my heart pounding, and I wheezed toward the summit where Coach Halpin waited, chewing his gum.

"That's good," he would say. And I would swoon.

At home, I checked the progress of my calves in the bathtub, and seeing no marked improvement, I pestered my dad into jogging with me on the weekends. He drove me to Hunt's Park in his Pinto, and he smoked a cigarette while I stretched. Then he slogged beside me on my long tedious turtle-paced lap, wearing red shorts that were too tight and too short and a bandanna tied Tonto-style around his balding head, and I would have been embarrassed except that I couldn't do it without him. If I was going to be a great Olympic champion, I'd need every advantage I could get, and Dad stayed with it, against all odds, plodding beside me week after week in plain view of normal families playing and picnicking and lounging on the grass. Sometimes we stopped at Dairy Queen on the way home.

After a while, Dad became sort of the unofficial assistant coach. He couldn't always make practice because of work, but he came to the Saturday meets. The distance races came last, so I had time to kill, hours of it, and I spent that time stretching and gawking at Coach's legs. My dad stretched with me for as long as he could, leaning out over his belly, reaching for his toes—loitering like the nice boy who has a crush on you and follows you around like a lost puppy, but whom you will never love, never in a million years—until duty called. His job was to wrangle kids back to the track when they inevitably wandered off. Those kids were not, in my view, serious runners. Not like Coach Halpin wanted us to be. They were sprinters after all, who spent ten seconds on the track, then the rest of the morning goofing around. My dad joked with them as they swung from the bleachers and searched for lost balls outside the tennis court fence. He would have liked me to join them, I think. But I would not stray. I stretched alone on the chalky football field through so many races—the 100's then 220's then 440's then 880's—waiting. When at last the starters called the mile, I toed the starting line at the farthest end, the slowest runners' spot, and I craned my neck to make sure Coach Halpin was watching. He always was. He leaned out from the bleachers with a palm-sized silver stopwatch on a string around his neck while I ran, pumping my fists furiously, willing myself through one excruciating lap then the next.

"Kick," he hollered for the last hundred yards or so. "Kick for the finish!"

And by god I kicked.

"Doing good," my dad hollered. "That's my girl," he said.

And I cringed.

I lost races by dramatic margins, trailing the leaders by a full five minutes, usually getting lapped in a one-mile race, and there my dad would be at the finish line with a hug. No chastisement. No technical hints for improvement. My dad seemed destined to be one lousy Olympic parent. He seemed too laid back. After the meet he'd take my hand to walk across miles of parking lots to the

Pinto, and I'd turn for one last fleeting look at Coach Halpin the way a girl in a movie does to signal to the audience the plot to come, the plot they know by heart: that eventually she will leave one boy for another.

A few years later, when I was a teenager lying on my bedroom floor listening to Jackson Browne and rehashing the mysteries of love, I decided Coach Halpin had been my first. My first love and, as it turns out, my first heartbreak. I had adored him, had wanted so badly to impress him, and one day when I least expected it, everything changed.

It was September when Coach Halpin invited me to a cross-country race, something entirely new, in the mountains. He and his wife owned a cabin at Lake Arrowhead, he told my parents, and they wondered if I might join them for the weekend. It was a big deal. I didn't often leave home overnight. I ran the race in the morning after a brief rain squall, pounding along the highway through the glistening pines, my feet slapping the wet pavement as the sun broke through the trees at intervals and splintered into separate blinding rays. I ran into sunlight and back out again alone, the very last runner at the back of the pack, and Coach Halpin stood at the end of the ribboned finish chute to congratulate me. Right then, I was still happy to see him.

After the race, we drove through the woods to his cabin, which I had pictured as magical, palatial even, and entered a too-small house littered with mismatched folding chairs and dog-eared copies of *Readers Digest*. The trouble had begun. His wife prepared a soup with an unpleasant foreign smell for dinner—lentils, I think they were—and I found a bay leaf in my bowl, a hard inedible thing afloat on brothy mush. Then Coach changed out of his running shorts, and I didn't like seeing him that way. Regular clothes made him look old, I thought, and shabby, less than what he ought to be. I swallowed my soup as best I could and waited for dessert that never came. Then, the final straw, they switched on the television, and we watched the Miss America Contest. Girls swaggered across the screen in their swimsuits, and to me they looked distinctly weak—sissies, sissies, sissies!—undeserving of attention, particularly attention from Coach Halpin. I tried to feign interest, tried at least to keep my eyes open, but I failed. I was exhausted.

Sometimes I think it was tiredness, finally, that caused everything to change. But it wasn't just that. There was a new hardness in me when I woke in that strange house. I missed the softer spot, the wanting. I had loved Coach Halpin, not this musty-house man with the strange food and the TV girls. On the way back home, I got carsick and threw up all over the backseat.

As a teenager, I turned the hurt over and over in my mind, examining it like a cleverly wrapped present, like an obsession. Nothing had happened, nothing at all, but everything had changed, and I wanted to know why. I wanted to make sense of it because I feared, rightly, it was the kind of thing that might happen to me again: one day love, next day nausea. It might happen to anyone, at any time, without warning, and because of that, it seemed inevitable and maddeningly unreasonable. I told myself it was the worst kind of hurt that you could experience or cause. I was wrong.

I kept running for a while out of habit, I suppose, and Dad would come after work to pick me up. He brought a stopwatch, and sometimes he brought his shorts and ran with us, though he did not stay long in the back of the pack with me. He charged ahead with the older kids, the eighth-grade boys that Coach Halpin allowed to join us then, near the end of my short-lived career, with the shadow of mustaches on their lips and gigantic formless quadriceps. Dad had, by then, lost some weight and quit smoking and bought a shelf full of books about running. He was training for a half-marathon. In hindsight, I guess I can see that he had grown a little fanatical. At the time, I didn't think about him much.

One afternoon my mom dropped me off. She had given me special dispensation from my religious education classes so I wouldn't miss practice. That's how serious it had become. I stood on the curb as she pulled away, then I dawdled as I weaved through the neighborhood to the place where a break in a chainlink fence opened out into the hills where we practiced. I looked through the break, a jagged porthole of torn and misshapen metal, and I could see Coach Halpin balancing on one foot flamingo-style with his other foot pulled up behind him, stretching his quad. From where I stood, he looked impossibly skinny and sinister, like a thief. I looked at the hills that I was supposed to run, and I thought I might come back someday all grown up and run over them as easily as flying, the way I did in my dreams, stroking my arms through the air like a swimmer. I looked at the hills, then I turned and studied the row of stoplights, red yellow green, staggered out along California Street, the long road back home. I don't remember deciding. I do remember how it felt to sprint, like the final strides of a long race, how ungraceful I was in triumph with my head lolling back across my shoulders and my chest thrust forward, dragging my legs along. I ran all the way home.

When I got home, my father faced me alone. He was angry.

"Why?" he asked. Why hadn't I been at practice? If I didn't want to go, why hadn't I just told them so?

He had stopped by after work to pick me up, and I was nowhere to be found; they had been worried that something terrible had happened. Now he stood before me, long past dinner time, not even having changed out of his suit from work. His loosened tie hung off-center at his chest. He hesitated.

"Was it too hard?" he asked.

I shook my head. Of course it was not too hard. Running was the easiest thing.

Years later, my mother would try to explain it to me. Running, by then, would not be an easy subject for us to broach. They had worried, she told me, that they had pressured me too much.

"Then why?" my dad asked.

I shifted my weight from foot to foot, and I cried a bit. I didn't have an answer. I don't remember feeling pressured, though I don't think I knew what that meant. I remember that I looked at Coach

Halpin one day and he was not what I had thought he was. And how do you explain that to your dad? I fell silent, and my chest pulled tight as a drum.

I quit running after that. I imagine I spent my time attending slumber parties and watching *Monkees* reruns on TV and listening to my transistor radio, waiting to hear my favorite songs. I played a little tennis. My dad bought me *Young Athlete* magazines, and I taped pictures of the cutest boys to my bedroom wall. I taped up Bjorn Borg, and I taped up Dwight Stones, the great American high jumper with feathered blond surfer hair, famous for wearing Mickey Mouse T-shirts. I loved Dwight Stones. I wanted to be like him. My dad took me to Goodwill to buy a mattress, then to the lumber yard for posts that we'd set in paint cans of cement, then, finally, to the river bottom to cut an eight-foot bamboo pole for the bar so I could practice high jumping in the backyard. Then, inevitably, I started going to track meets.

My backyard pit served me well. We attended a long series of meets, my dad and me, and I collected a box of ribbons, many of them blue. I was tall for my age, though that would change soon enough when all my classmates would shoot up past me and laugh me away from high-school basketball tryouts. At ten I was tall. And I could jump. I had taught myself the Fosbury flop, the backwards-over-the-bar Dwight Stones way to jump, and a skill that obscure gives a fifth-grader some advantage. What freedom there was in soaring face upturned to the sun, then somersaulting wildly, backwards, onto the big blue mat. No eternal plodding, this, but an exuberant surge, an explosion of hope. I went to watch my dad run his half-marathon in some foggy distant hills, and when I met him in the finish chute, there was no hint of his familiar unmitigated glee, only exhaustion and no small measure of relief. He checked his wristwatch as I hugged his waist, then he bent to catch his breath, and I was so glad to have abandoned endurance. High jumping was so easy and so much my own. I felt strong and independent. I taught my dog Junior to jump over the bamboo pole at its lowest heights, and I could spend hours in the backyard alone with my dog, reveling in my newfound passion, my very own passion, and I could pretend not to notice when my dad was away, out running or, more often, at the hospital—he was having some kind of health problems—and on Saturdays, we could still hit the road, me and Dad. We went to one meet, then the next, and I just kept winning.

Eventually, we ended up at the state age-group championships, at a larger stadium somewhere near Los Angeles, a full stadium, with a rubber track rather than a dirt one. There was noise in the stands, excitement, and I made my way up through the competition, easily clearing one height then the next. When I approached the bar at four-foot-four, it was higher than I'd ever jumped before. It was taller than I was at the time. I ran the semicircle approach, then leapt and arched back into that elaborate airborne backbend and kicked my legs in unison at just the right moment and landed in the huge mat gazing up at the bar. It did not so much as quiver. The fact that I missed at the next height three times in a row didn't matter. I had won third place in the state for fifth-grade girls—a bronze medal!—and during the awards ceremony my dad jumped over the wall from the stands and ran across the rubber track to wrap me in a bear hug. It's one of the clearest memories I have of him. He died a year later of a heart attack while out running, just collapsed there on the sidewalk in his shorts and sneakers and the dorky bandanna. His heart surgeon had told him to give it up after the quadruple bypass. No running, the surgeon said, but my dad didn't listen. Sometimes I am angry. Sometimes I wish I could stand before him alone and ask just this: Why?

At the state meet, they broadcast my name over a loudspeaker when they awarded the medal. I listened to it echo through the crowd, and though I hadn't thought of him in months, I suddenly wished that Coach Halpin were there. I wished he could watch me stand upon the makeshift platform with a medal draped around my neck. I wished it the way you wish revenge. There, I thought, I

showed you. I did it without you. See! See! I did it all by myself! I
thought this even though it was patently untrue. And while I was
thinking this, right in the middle of it, my dad jumped over the
railing. He vaulted actually, like a younger, more agile version of
himself, and he sprinted across the track nearly interrupting a race
in progress. He lifted me in his arms and spun me around as if I'd
scored the winning touchdown. I remember it clearly, and I
remember it with something like regret, something like shame, for
the way that memory, like love, sometimes clings to all the wrong
things. I have precious few memories of my father. I wish like heck
I spent more of my Jackson Browne hours holding fast to those
memories, nurturing them for posterity, instead of dwelling on
Coach Halpin. Inside that package of hurt that obsessed me so much
was something, after all, as common as dirt. I fell out of love, out
of infatuation probably, out of a plain little girl crush, for godssake.
Why doesn't matter a whit. What we learn and what we keep are
the prizes.

My running career, short-lived though it was, left me a few.
There's a dusty shoebox in a closet at my mother's house with a
handful of ribbons and one third-place medal. There's loyalty and
tenacity and endurance, evidence that after all this time I am still
not fast, never will be, that I am, perhaps, made for distance. There
are memories of love, real and imagined, obsessive and
embarrassing, solid and lasting, cheering from the sidelines and
then running beside me and then passing me by, moving on to
places I cannot reach, driven by motives I cannot understand. There
are a couple pair of cheap running shoes in my closet at any given
time, since I still run occasionally, casually, to stay in shape. And
there are Coach Halpin's calves, now my own. They are hard stony
knobs, sculpted and gaudy and embarrassingly out of proportion
to my smallish frame, and I am not always proud of them, but I am
stronger because of them—stronger than I ever dreamed of being—
and it's a probably a damned good thing because, when you're
eight, you can never dream how strong you'll have to be.

The Doodles We Draw

I am still wet from the shower and fumbling to dress when they approach.
The other girls from fourth-period P.E. are all big hair and menace.

"Ana Maria," they call. They surround me and pose like a heavy metal band, fists jabbed into bony hips, lips curled into practiced sneers.

"We think you'd look good in make-up," they say. It's a lie, I know, but I have no choice. They are already wielding lipstick tubes like light sabers.

"Ana Maria," they call again at their sing-songy loudest, even though I am right there in front of them, even though there's no place I could go even if I wanted to. I glance toward the exit. There is only one way out, and lunch period is next so no one will be coming in.

I daydreamed my way through high school, through Algebra II and Spanish III and even Morality class, doodling fir trees on my Pee Chee folders. I wore a ragg wool sweater that I ordered from L.L. Bean with my babysitting money, and I strummed John Denver painstakingly, incessantly, on my nylon-stringed guitar. In an autobiography for confirmation class, I listed backpacking as one of my hobbies even though my friend, Dawn, the cheerleader, died laughing because she'd been backpacking more often than I had, which was exactly once. I was a nerd, a self-made nerd of the highest order. There was not another ragg wool sweater, I think, in all of my hometown. Mostly because the temperature there rarely drops below sixty degrees. I was shameless, sure, but never hopeless.

Over my bed I pasted a religious poster showing a backpacker wandering over a mountain pass with the King James inscription: *Behold I am with thee and will keep thee wherever thou goest.*

It all began the summer after eighth grade when the parents of a toddler I babysat invited me on a road trip to the Oregon coast, ostensibly to babysit, but probably because they could see that I could use a trip. I was the oldest child in my now single-parent family, hyper-responsible and falsely mature. Three weeks would be the longest I'd ever spent away from home, and I'd spend it in the overcrowded cab of a battered Ford truck with an eight-track tape player. I'd spend it camping and chasing after the toddler and ogling at mountains and moss, at fast-running streams and windblown firs on the beach. Outside Tillamook, we detoured up a logging road to a waterfall and stepped out in a drizzle that settled in droplets on my sweatshirt sleeves. I'd never seen such a thing. Over the next four years, I could conjure that moment perfectly, too perfectly sometimes, during Sunday Mass or a history test.

The rest of high school life raced past me in a bewildering blur: clothes and makeup and dances and cars and other more mysterious things, things not to mention to the girl who plays guitar faithfully in the church choir. I let it race by. Because no one invited me to drink beer, because I didn't have the slightest idea what to say to boys I had crushes on, I buried myself in schoolwork and sports.

When for P.E. we were assigned to play badminton for a month, I threw myself at that. Dawn and I practiced in her garage on weekends among the boxes of Rice-A-Roni (a lifetime supply) her mom had won on her latest game show appearance. We remained neck and neck in the P.E. badminton tournament, diving for shots and skidding across the gym floor while the other girls whined and tested the limits of the no-sitting-on-the-bleachers-and-gossiping rule. But on the last day of the badminton tournament, Dawn was home sick, so I won handily. I didn't notice the other girls' disgust until it was too late.

"Why don't you wear make-up?" one of the girls demands, "hmmm?" Her voice rises a full octave. "Why not?"

What am I supposed to say? Because I don't know how to wear make-up, for one thing. Because I'm scared of that dress-up world. Because I'm safer here with my John Denver and my mossy dreams. I am silent.

Outside, a rare winter rainstorm begins to pelt the metal roof of the locker room while my classmates cackle and smear my face with lipstick and rouge and thick black eyeliner scribbles of humiliation. Margaret Kessler, the girl with Pat Benatar looks and crusty scars from trying to pierce her own nose in the girls' bathroom, gets particularly vicious. She slathers my cheeks with Max Factor 12 then sweeps the mascara wand back and forth windshield-wiper style across my scrunched-up eyes. But it is a group effort, and it lasts a long time, it seems, this frenzied art project, before they are finally bored or repentant enough to wander away.

When they are finished, I wash my face, scrubbing off teary cosmetic gobs with hot water and paper towels. Then I sprint out the door, past the in-crowd at the snack bar with their diet Cokes and Twinkies, past my nerdy friends with their brown bag lunches at the picnic tables, past the teacher guarding the gate while his back is turned, and out, running through the rain, soaking my beloved sweater until it stinks like a wet dog, down the quiet midday streets and home to my bedroom, door slammed, alone, with my music, and my poster. *Wherever thou goest.* I am O.K. I am pretty darned sure I'll get out someday.

These days I inhabit pretty closely that world I dreamed. Yesterday the dew from an overnight thunderstorm settled on the sleeves of my cotton shirt as I hiked up Park Creek, and I felt something like deja vu, not for the thousands of times the dew has settled like that, but for the thousands of times I imagined it, more real than the real thing. Times like that I wonder if sometimes memory works backwards, if we can remember the future. Maybe it wasn't outlandish fantasy all those years, but some kind of prescience that kept me outfitted in hiking boots on the sidewalk. Sometimes I'm almost certain of it.

A couple years ago I managed to sort through some things in my old bedroom. There was a wall-sized imitation Pac Man advertisement I painted in art class. There was a Carter/Mondale campaign poster. And there it was: the backpacker heading over the mountain pass. I looked at it closely. For a second it looked a little bit like Cascade Pass, the most popular trail I work on. It couldn't be. Then I looked again. Well, it just might be. When I got out my own snapshots to compare, there was no doubt left at all: it was Cascade Pass. It was more than coincidence, I think, but what it was, exactly, I'm still not sure. I rolled the poster back up and shoved it back behind the bedpost.

ᴈᴈ

Shortly after the Oregon road trip, my friends gave birth to a second daughter, and chose me to be her godmother. When I was not in my dream world, I was happiest romping in her baby world, then her two- and three-year-old world, until finally I graduated and headed north, at last, to Oregon for college. Next year she graduates from high school. Sometimes I am tempted to write to her and tell her what I've learned, if I can figure it out.

Who knows what my teenaged self thought I'd find in the mountains? Something different. Some cleaner air, some new version of myself, unnerdy and capable. I don't want to tell my goddaughter that nature will save her, to go out now and buy a ragg wool sweater. She'd never go for it, anyway. She is no Grape Nut, but a city girl of sorts, full of grace and poise, who gets good grades, goes to church, and wears make-up tastefully.

What I want to tell her is something more, something greeting card cliché: to hold fast to her dreams, whatever they might be. I want to tell her that they very well might come true, but that even if they don't, dreams, like faith, are worth every bit as much while you're dreaming them as when they come true. There is safety in the doodles we draw. And there is hope.

Doing Without

৻৶

I want to make one thing clear from the get-go: I am an environmentalist.
If it came down to it—wilderness or death—I'd chain myself to a
fir tree, lie in the path of bulldozers, start attending gun shows,
whatever it would take. Note the if. It's not death yet, at least not
for the eight hundred thousand or so acres of wilderness that
surround me now. It's just life and how to live it.

For now, I'm living in a friend's summer cabin. It's November,
and I'm burning a lot of clear Douglas fir—the kind that sells in
Japan for more American dollars per tree than I earn in a year—
that has sat at the bottom of a woodshed for a decade. I cook on a
woodstove, shower in wood-heated water, use an outhouse. I was
laid off from my job on the trail crew a month ago so I'm sleeping
late, pinching pennies, and reading a lot. That's why I'm writing
this. What I'm reading embarrasses me.

Outside magazine, for starters, followed by collections of literary
nature essays, and then, the final straw, newsletters from
conservation organizations. In every case, I'm put off by the
message: Don't cut down trees. Don't maintain roads. Don't give
in to encroaching technology. The plain bossiness is, to me,
wincingly familiar.

In grade school, I collected Good Citizenship awards by the
drawerful. I tiptoed along the straight and narrow, unreasonably
terrified of punishment and unfailingly certain of the rewards down
the road in high school, then in college, in church, then maybe in
heaven. Don't do anything, I figured, and you won't do anything
wrong. I did my homework and said my prayers. I worried myself

into frenzies, then took it out on others. By all indications, I was an environmentalist in the making.

Where did it get me, all that exemplary behavior? Got me here, I try to remember. And it's a good life. I'm taking long walks, tromping across a soggy, decomposing mat of big-leaf maple leaves, the size and texture of notebook paper. I'm watching for the clouds to shatter apart as they do every few days so I can watch winter teasing its way down, the snow line leaving a clear demarcation—green and white—at the freezing level as it moves from one thousand feet above the valley floor, to six hundred, then three, and back up again. If it weren't for environmentalists, I'd probably be sitting in a clear-cut or along a state highway. So what is it about my allies that makes me cringe?

Exaggeration, for one thing. We're so vigilant watching for blatant nature crimes—windblown mining tailings, half-a-state clear-cuts, wetlands-turned-shopping malls—that we sometimes blow things all out of proportion. Thinning, the necessary logging of some trees in order to allow tangled and lightless would-be forests to grow more successfully, becomes the work of "timber beasts." (This, a direct quote from one of the newsletters strewn angrily across my bedroom floor.) Collecting gravel from the small, plentifully supplied pit near my home becomes "strip mining." (This, too.) We've become insufferable tattletales, too eager to expose wrongdoings, however minor. There is a subtle self-righteousness to even our best environmental intentions.

Tread lightly. This, in a nutshell, is the wilderness message. Take only pictures. Leave only footprints. Don't build a campfire. Don't bring a dog. The immaculately maintained bulletin board flyers in the national park where I work, as in many others I've visited, warn against: rattlesnakes, ticks, Giardia, grizzly bears, and fishing without a license. Nature is packaged up as potential breaches of courtesy and potential dangers, much as life was when we were children. Don't cross the street without looking both ways. Don't talk with your mouth full. This idea that our own good manners can save the planet is self-centered in a way that, say, a cougar could never imagine being. Granted, the cougar has fewer choices. But the power to choose, we're squandering it, I think, on the mundane.

I realize I'm being awfully rough on my younger self. Outside of school, outside anywhere, I was something else altogether. I climbed trees, shot baskets, slammed tennis balls against the garage door. I spun circles up one driveway and down the next on a skateboard between sitcom reruns on TV. I had enormous uncontained energy.

Later, in adolescence, the energy turned to restlessness, a vague physical longing that I assumed had something to do with sex, and surely it did, but which was a hunger for something more than that, too. I stood on the rim of the Grand Canyon on one family vacation, snapping photos and trying to shake the sinking feeling that I was destined to experience life from behind a pane of glass— a camera lens, a TV screen, a windshield. I wanted to wallow in the stuff of life—dirt, water, sunlight—but didn't think I'd ever get to do it. The world was, I decided, all screwed up.

Turns out, I now know, that it wasn't just me. Most environmentalists feel the same. There's an apocalyptic desperation that makes us believe along with the survivalists and the New Agers that it's all gonna be gone soon. It's the kind of desperation that makes *Into the Wild*, the story of the suburban kid shirking modern life only to die in an abandoned city bus in Alaska, a bestseller. With hopelessness as the alternative, it's no wonder that environmentalists of the last generation sunk in their claws and fought with religious fervor for wilderness, for places where people could throw on a knapsack and march right out of the screwiness. It's no wonder, either, that they began to legislate rules of increasing stringency: no logging, no mining, no roads, then no chainsaws, no campfires. Such behavior must have seemed like the only way to survive. In wildness, to paraphrase Thoreau, is the preservation of ourselves.

❧

One spring morning in college I awoke with a severe case of diarrhea that would last nearly three years. I forced down slices of dry toast that curdled and moaned in my intestines. Sipped water. Studied through the gauzy web of hunger. Eventually I went to see doctors who ran inconclusive tests and referred me to psychiatrists. Determined to tough it out on my own, I turned to my childhood code of *don't*. I read books about diet that convinced me that so many foods were bad for me that I dropped almost all of them. Caffeine, alcohol, and sugar at first. Easy enough. Then, as time went by: meat, wheat, dairy products, spicy foods, citrus. Predictably, I began to wither—120, 110, 100 pounds, and less.

The various go-without diets were not without their inconveniences, but the health food store carries items for every diet imaginable. It was a whole lot harder trying to figure out what I could eat. None of the rules ever seemed to apply. Something from nearly every category was OK, something was not. Cheese, but not milk. Spinach, but not green beans. Poultry, but not pork.

My stomach eventually, miraculously, healed itself. Maybe the microorganism died off. Maybe I broke the code, the test foods finally falling into perfect balance. I had moved to the woods by then, and maybe a summer of work outdoors made me forget about the ailment long enough for it to heal. Even at the height of my diet obsession, I had begun to suspect that the fixation was less healthy than a bacon cheeseburger. Don't get me wrong. I am still convinced that the sickness was in my stomach, not my psyche. It's not the sickness that I'm questioning now, but the zeal for purity.

Of course, environmentalists don't hold the lease on extremism. Some of our neighbors resent any suggestion that they can't do with the land whatever they please. ("I have two kinds of land," says one. "Land that's been cleared and land that's gonna be cleared.") They are quick to point out familiar hypocrisies. Usually, they say, environmental arguments are made by people from the city, by climbers who stab flags in sacred mountains, by skiers who pay to scar over alpine meadows. Usually the arguments are composed on computers, submitted by fax, accepted by phone, edited by e-mail, and eventually, discussed over freshly ground coffee. Usually they center on what we've been doing wrong out here—Nothing! the neighbors cry, Nothing at all!—and what we should not be doing. The neighbors, red faced, demand an opposing sort of asceticism: Don't question the rights of private property owners. Don't even mention spotted owls.

About a mile down the road, Walter G. Winkel harbors genuine concerns about space aliens taking over the world. To his mind, it would not be much different, I suppose, from what happened in his lifetime here, with the National Park Service assuming jurisdiction of nearly all the acres of forest surrounding his. His few acres are littered freely with junk (to Wally an organized inventory): old cars, spare tires, salvaged lumber and plumbing fixtures, compost heaps, and always, the huge fir rounds in preparation for winter. On Friday nights, he starts a campfire—"a smudge," he calls it—and a few coworkers and friends, regulars all, sit on rounds to drink some beer and exchange news and get an earful of Wally's tall tales and accumulated wisdom. He can predict with accuracy which of the steep drainages into the valley will flood, which won't. He knows which plants have medicinal properties, and he grows the most brilliant and vigorous tulips in the valley. Despite his wacky fears, Wally can make me feel like an apprentice to an environmental tradition that is alive outside the pages of glossy magazines and trade paperbacks.

The knowledge grows incrementally that nature is never one-dimensional—all this and none of that. Audubon calendars don't show the half of it. At some point up here, the superlative views go occasionally unnoticed. The pounding of waterfalls in spring grows almost annoying. You've lost something, then. But gained something too. You split open a round of old-growth fir with a twelve-pound sledge and metal wedges and there in the heartwood you see the message: growth, resilience, and in the end, usefulness. Used as warmth for my family gathered at the Thanksgiving table next week, as fuel for cooking the turkey, as hot water for rinsing wine glasses, for a late-night shower. The lessons I culled from my pious upbringing—to forgive, to share what you have, to keep the faith—aren't too much different from what I've learned from a decade in these woods—to remember that things heal, to leave a little of what you take, and, always, to endure.

I admit that I am sometimes a lousy environmentalist. Those gun conventions, if I started going to them, I'd be going for the same reason everyone else does. Because I'd want to protect the way I live my life. I care less about saving the resources for future generations than I do about knowing I'm living fully, indulgently, in a place where things make sense to me. Over time, I've learned a healthy, sometimes vicious, distrust of *don't*.

Maybe that's all I want to say to *Outside*, to the Sierra Club: 'fess up. Just admit it and drop the pretense. Saving the environment can be a mask for wanting to be in it ourselves. There's not a damned thing wrong with that. So why not lighten up? Climbers can drag their ropes to the summit if they want. Wally can leave that junk in his yard. I'll sit in this summer cabin, heated ferociously by old-growth Douglas fir by the cordful, drinking strong coffee with half-and-half by the quartful, waiting, ever vigilant, because tomorrow the snow might finally drift down into the yard, and I'll stumble outside to spin gleeful purposeless circles, overcome with giddiness, knowing with certainty that caring for nature, like caring for ourselves, is more complex and dire than just doing without.

Choir Practice

❧

I went to Catholic Mass every Sunday of my childhood. But it's not like
you think. My early memories of church are of wide outdoor, windy,
sometimes hot affairs, always sunny and always led by a group of
young men and women wearing bright clothes and toting blocky
guitars. The Circle of Joy, they called themselves. They must have
been in their early twenties. And they stood there with no shame,
singing exuberant three-chord hymns: *Shout from the Highest
Mountain, Kumbaya, To Be Alive.* Their hair draped down around
their shoulders or down to their waists, to where their brightly
colored smocks met their Levis. It's easy now to groan, to ridicule
their unfashionable earnestness. I do it all the time. But when I
was five, six, seven years old the excitement was palpable.

The beauty of outdoor Mass was that we never had to sit still. My
younger sister and I reveled in the freedom. We danced, spinning
wildly, kicking out the pleats of our sundresses, or we sprinted across
the grounds of the historic California ranch that the Divine Word
Missionaries used as a seminary. Never mind that "The Sem," as our
parents called it, sat nestled in dry hills that burned annually and
were threaded by eroded fire access roads. The grounds themselves,
where Mass was said, were lush and enticing. They included shallow
lily ponds stocked with goldfish. Once, with no better excuse than
curiosity, my sister and I tossed our baby brother into a pond, then
sobbed all the way home when our parents refused to make the ritual
stop at Winchell's Donut Shop. The grounds also included acres of
orange groves, enough acres that we could drive our parents to
distraction by chanting "orange groves, orange groves, orange
groves" for the ten or fifteen minutes it took to drive through them.

Sometimes during or after Mass we visited Mary. We rolled somersaults down the lawn toward the orange groves, and then took a hard left and hiked in the shade of pungent eucalyptus trees to where the eternal Virgin stood—chipped paint over cement—looking down at us lovingly. We hung on her for a few bored moments then tromped back up toward the happy music.

One Easter morning one of the bearded guitarists loped up the hill from the orange groves interrupting the opening hymn to announce dramatically that Jesus had risen out there—Right There!—and in my six-year-old mind, there was nothing the least bit odd about the fact that God himself had waited two thousand years to come back to life in the dry foothills of a Los Angeles suburb. I had awakened to more chocolate than I'd ever seen in my life, and I'd landed in the fanciest dress I'd ever worn, on a sunny morning in the orange groves with all the people I loved the most. Jesus. Why not? Who wouldn't want to be here? I believed without articulating it, without needing to, that heaven lay somewhere out in that sweet-smelling expanse—orange groves, orange groves, orange groves—the kind of place where Jesus could roll back the rock of his tomb, change into grubby Levis and scoop up a nylon-string guitar. Who would need anything more?

Eventually, predictably, all efforts to recruit and educate new priests in the Divine Word proved futile. The Sem became a lovely nursing home for aging missionaries from around the world. The Circle of Joy splintered, victims of their own aging, I suppose, or of changes in the church, in politics, in culture, the pendulum swinging right. Adults in their late twenties weren't supposed to sing so loudly, so hopefully. The last time I remember them singing together was at my father's funeral, where Jackie Peterson led the chorus to "Day by Day" from *Godspell*, complete with soaring harmonies, hand clapping, and a lengthy tambourine solo, while I pretended my eleven-year-old tears were an allergic reaction to the incense the priest burned over the coffin.

Remaining members of the Circle of Joy moved, as my family did, to a more traditional local church that looked a lot like a bank. Our Lady's Savings and Loan, neighbors called it. The choir, as they were now generically known, sang increasingly complex and occasionally somber songs. Their hair crept up their necks, and their clothes grew less colorful, even as their voices and guitar strumming grew more sophisticated. Sometime around this time, I decided, wildest of wild hairs, to spend all my babysitting money on a guitar. The choir allowed me to hover at rehearsals on the outskirts of the former Circle, watching their fingers, listening to their harmonies, strumming off beat, every Tuesday evening for six years. I never grew to know the choir members well, was too young to follow the forces that shaped them, that drew them together then one at a time sent them away.

Jackie Peterson and Pat Miller were the de facto leaders of the choir. The two women, creeping up on thirty by this time, were the most dedicated and talented of the musicians, and they were, in many ways, polar opposites. Pat was, well, masculine, heavyset and muscular with short brown hair and the hint of a mustache. She sang lower than a tenor, closer to baritone, in perfect harmony with Jackie. She dressed up in corduroy jeans on Christmas, and she drove a truck for a living. "Is that a man or a woman?" children in the church pews sniggered, though they knew the truth. Even the androgynous name was a stumper. I wondered about it myself, secretly, genuinely. Why would a woman look and act so much like a man? The strangeness repulsed me, though I cringe to admit it now, and though I knew even then that repulsion was not an acceptable reaction to anyone, especially someone at church. Besides, I loved Pat. We all did. She was the kindliest member of the choir, its spiritual if not musical centerpiece. She joked with me freely when I missed chord changes and followed my high-school swim-team career loyally. When it came time for me to leave, she and Kelly organized a surprise graduation party.

It had been years earlier, while I was still lost in family grief, that Pat had begun to spend time with Kelly, a divorcée, ten or twelve years her senior, with five kids. Though I had a good idea of the nature of their relationship, I maintained a solid wordless loyalty that separated the sexual from the social. It wasn't much different from the way I separated the dirty method of making babies—the method Susie Beckwith described to me on the playground—from the other more ethereal one, the one my parents had surely used. I'd read about homosexuals, had heard the ribald jokes, but Pat and Kelly were to me something else, something comfortably unspoken, something less visceral. My mom invited them to our home each Christmas Day, that empty fatherless curse of a holiday, and they always, without fail, brought thoughtful personalized gifts that they probably could not afford. Mom referred to them, on Christmas as the rest of the year, in the same blended syllable she used for any married couple we knew— "Pennyn'Joe," "Jann'Mike," "Patn'Kelly." She even turned her back when we visited their home, allowing my sister and me to sneak glimpses of the double bed they shared. Kelly's divorce-scarred kids were less tolerant. "If I ever catch her doing those things to my mom," they said, "I'll kill her." When they said these things, I'd turn away, allowing myself no mental pictures, thinking only this: Shut Up.

Jackie was more talented than Pat, more feminine, and much more aloof. She worked in the Women's Center at the local university and had taken in recent years to wearing fashionable blazers, very academic, usually adorned with a political button of some variety: Stop Rape Now. Or just: N. O. W. I watched Jackie's fingers most closely, and I admired her new expensive round-backed guitar. I swooned when she'd lay her head back and let her powerful alto run its full leash. I privately agreed when churchgoers likened her voice to Karen Carpenter's, though Jackie herself detested the comparison, and I smarted, rather than laughed, when

I failed to meet her moody expectations. One afternoon, we were rehearsing for a wedding. (They allowed me to participate even on these paid occasions, splitting the money evenly so that my cloddy strumming drew the same twenty or thirty dollars that Jackie's trained fingers did.) Jackie was teaching a harmony, repeating it over and over. Though I did not even pretend to sing, the guitar taking all my concentration, I anticipated the moment when Jackie would wander out into the empty pews to listen to the merging voices cascade off the high ceiling, and the only guitar, the only one, would be my own. I strummed mightily, dragging a heavy plastic pick across thick nylon strings, almost hitting it right, just about getting the timing down. Jackie let out a sigh, and marched back toward the podium. When she reached it, she wove through the singers, toward the back—toward me, I slowly realized—and she placed her hand flat against the strings of my guitar. She could not even joke, as Pat surely would have, about me thinking I was the star. Just one single silencing motion.

On another, more perplexing, Tuesday evening, I loitered as usual behind the remnants of the Circle of Joy with my own music stand. A kindly middle-aged man, a short-lived member, was teaching me blues riffs between the hymns. Meanwhile, Jackie, up front, was more animated than usual, describing a situation at work.

"They are flagrant," she complained.

I strained to eavesdrop while I stumbled through a blues progression in E.

"This one woman, Sylvia, walks by my desk, leans down on both elbows, and asks me to convert. Then …" Jackie paused with exaggerated disgust. "Then, she kisses the top of my head." Jackie's voice echoed through the darkened church for her punchline: "Keep your lesbian perversions to yourself!"

Jackie claimed to have said it. Now she repeated it, over and over, so loudly that the microphone squawked and whined in rebellion.

"Keep your lesbian perversions to yourself!"

I stole a glance at Pat and Kelly who were both laughing, and I felt angry and confused and gravely embarrassed. I walked the six suburban blocks home by streetlight, still fuming, still uncertain in my naiveté why such words needed to exist, and wondering what sort of fear or meanness might have forced Jackie to use them like weapons. I replayed the scene in my mind so often—Jackie's voice so unnecessarily loud, so uncharacteristically edgy and grating—that over time, and with some sympathy, I came to recognize the distinct tone of denial. With no particular surprise I learned, a few years later, after I had long since left California and stopped attending Catholic Mass anywhere, that Sylvia and Jackie had become lovers.

Sometimes when I return home to visit my mother, I attend Mass with her. There in the Savings and Loan, I feel the warmth that underscored those Tuesday rehearsals flood back over me. There in the dark, between hymns, was the chance to think on Things Larger. There also was the intimacy that grows from the mutual thinking upon Things Larger. I try to analyze it now. I wrack my queerly educated brain to determine if those years carried the allure of sexuality, if my attraction to the church, to those women, was somehow physical. If it was, I did not know it. And if it was, it was the safest of sexuality: a comfort zone where what I wore and what I said were accepted without ridicule, where the sadness of having lost my father so young found an outlet and an explanation and a community. I suppose those years carried the seed of Lesbianism to exactly the extent they carried the seed of Catholicism. They taught me some respect for the words, and some revulsion at the way the words—Lesbian, Catholic—could be twisted grotesquely to include and exclude, to judge and to humiliate. What Jackie and Pat and half a dozen other rotating choir members taught me most was beyond either word: their love encompassed me, gave me faith in the memory and the promise of joy.

The promise would be fulfilled a few years later when, by pure happenstance, I discovered my own more earthly paradise. I arrived by ferry, the only transportation available, in a tiny forested valley surrounded by rugged glaciated mountains, gorgeous beyond all reason. I settled into my summer job with an earnest shameless joy. I met other people my age—I turned twenty-three that summer—who shared my eagerness, and for the first time in my life, I became an extrovert. I hiked with clumps of strangers every weekend and attended nightly parties. I played in weekly softball games, diving for pop flies, taking full swing strikes, then connecting, driving long solid balls over the heads of unsuspecting outfielders. I met a roommate with whom I'd stay up all night sharing precious bottles of wine and deep intimate secrets. I wore shorts all summer, and come fall, only compromised to wearing shorts over long underwear, not wanting to admit any impending change. I had been offered an internship at an environmental journal—an enviable opportunity, I thought. On the full October moon, I sat alone on a bridge over the mountain river, shivering, playing my guitar and singing off key, trying to decide what to do. I returned to the cabin where my roommate awaited me. We had run out of wine and turned in shy desperation to Alka Seltzer cold medicine and cloves of baked garlic.

"Ever thought of staying the winter?" Laurie asked.

"I will if you will," I said.

From there it happened the usual way, over time, and with plenty of urgent drama, the truth becoming more apparent, and the two of us crying, crying, crying. One night I announced that I could not face it, that I was leaving for good, that I would hike out over the mountains, forget the damned ferry, and head for a straight and narrow career in journalism. In the morning, I lamely explained that I had stayed only because I could not find my boots. We admitted these crises to no one.

Sometime midwinter, after one night of platonic cuddling and one long week of fretting, we took a hard mutual swallow, the first of many, and blurted it out to a close male friend.

"We think we are in love," we said.

"It will never work," he said, "unless you use the L word."

"We just did use the L word," we said incredulously

We were not ready for that other word. Oh, we were ready for each other. We were even ready to let friends know, through pronoun or intimation, or by turning our backs while men whom one or the other of us had been dating only months prior glimpsed our double bed and scratched their heads. It was only the word and the dank and terrifying shadow it cast that we could not face. I would not be ready for another year or two, not until one afternoon when the phone rang in a drafty Victorian house in Missoula, Montana, where we lived for one winter.

I raced to get the phone for the fun of it.

"I have some bad news, Honey," my mom said. That's what she says when she's about to say someone died. She has known death too well and too often to mince words. "Jackie Peterson was brutally murdered."

Well, what was I supposed to say to that? I said, "Oh my God" because the words filled in the space while my mind traveled to that place on the edge of a cliff that I couldn't have looked down even if I tried. So I stepped away, to keep from falling, and I just kept saying, "Oh My God."

"I hope I'm not being a Pollyanna to say it," Mom said, "but Jackie's a martyr for her cause." She had been speaking out against domestic violence, working late at the Rape Crisis Center in Rialto. The killer left the phone in her hand to teach a lesson. Nobody would tell his girlfriend to leave him again. He beat her and raped her and gagged her with the sleeve of her blazer, then he tried to use her ATM card without a PIN number. The cops had film of him trying and retrying, but did not think they had a case. "Circumstantial evidence," Mom explained.

Mom said the funeral would be on Tuesday, at St. Francis. Mom didn't know if she would go. Jackie had never attended there. Jackie had long since stopped attending Our Lady, after the new missionary priest had, on a hunch, asked her and Sylvia to stop attending. Jackie's other friends, her friends from work, weren't going. They'd hold a service at Fairmount Park, Mom explained, though she didn't know if she'd go there either. "Those women are so aggressive," she said.

The body haunted me for a long time. Whenever I was still or silent for a moment, it would come into focus. All day long. All week long. Walking around town. Blazer in its mouth. At work. Phone in its hand. At home. Beaten beyond recognition. I tried versions of artistic exorcism: writing poems, playing hymns, begging, finally, aloud for Jackie to leave me alone. Instead, I became even more obsessive, replaying the murder incessantly in frantic detail. He beat her with the phone. He gagged her with her blazer. He raped her after she was dead. After she was dead!

Rialto, the grimy suburb where Jackie was killed, was where I'd seen my first pair of Nikes, the waffle stomp, the wave of things to come. My dad had taken me to see them. He had spent more money than I'd ever seen him spend right then and there, just to buy me those waffle-soled shoes. I could picture it still, Dad sliding the MasterCharge across the counter with a grin. I could picture another man many years later, with a cash card not his own, standing up to the camera at the ATM, standing there without the slightest fear of repercussion, never apparently having had to choose when or how to show himself to the world. The senselessness. The horrible fact that brute force could transcend the worrisome details of truth. I found myself thinking, unreasonably, that Rialto was a place for dead people. For ghosts. Just as for such a long time I had believed, unreasonably, that the word *lesbian* held some specific danger. About a week after Jackie's funeral, I broke the news. The poor long-distance connection crackled while Mom wept silently.

"Of course," she said, "I will always love you."

Now I mostly play my guitar when I am restless, when I am ready early for some appointment and I am waiting. There are certain patterns, certain simple finger-picking styles that I cannot play without the hair on the back of my neck standing up, as if I am calling Jackie back from the orange groves to take stock of my life—its necessary balance of truth and lies, silence and joy. Laurie and I live easily, charmed even, in this earthly paradise we call home. Our rural neighbors accept us with solid wordless loyalty. Our families love us. We do not attend church; we do not wear political buttons. Yes, yes, we're lesbians, we seem to say. But it's not like you think. If Jackie were here, I sometimes wonder if she'd look askance at this, our apolitical, areligious brand of integrity, and I am ashamed. Jackie taught me to tune my guitar. She taught me, by example, to stand straight and silent for the Gospel reading. She showed me how to read the harmony line, how dissimilar notes plait and meld into something more complicated, something that, once you get it right, can be so much more beautiful.

Several years after the murder, I do not hear her name very often. If I have any courage at all, I will ask Pat someday. I will phone her straight out of the blue. Mom must have the number. I will ask what happened to the killer, if he was ever brought to trial. I will ask her what happened to Jackie, when it began. With Sylvia? Or earlier, under the surface perhaps, with Pat? And where did it lead? Who did she become? I will ask what has happened to Pat and Kelly since they, too, have been asked to leave Our Lady. What do they believe? How do they forgive? Where do they find joy? I will ask and ask and ask, I swear it. For now, I am still strumming a few earnest chords. For now, I am still waiting for the old terrifying apparition—a body stripped and raped and gagged for eternity—to fade and give way to something wholly unexpected, a figure rising Christlike, against all odds, from the few orange groves left among the subdivisions: the image of a very young woman singing in the wind with her head laid back, her rich and agile voice belting out songs of hope—*to be alive and feeling free*—that will land on the waiting ears of small children somersaulting toward heaven.

On the Rim

ᘓ

Late fall in the Cascades. It had been raining for nearly three months, and we could fairly expect six months more. At work, tension among crew members neared the breaking point. At home, puddles spanned the dirt road along the river that I bicycled daily, the water rising to the pedals, then the sprocket. It was time to make a winter plan. I had known it before. I had known it the previous winter when I applied to graduate school—refuge for the aimless—but then I didn't get accepted, and eight months whizzed past and left me, by the time the alder leaves formed a slick mat on the drippy trail to the outhouse, sulking by the woodstove on my days off, plucking my guitar, rereading magazines months out of date. Another restless winter in the cedar shack felt too much like stagnation, like defeat. I needed to make money, but that wasn't the half of it. I was in the mood for escape, for adventure, for at least a new story to tell at work when tensions pulled guitar-string taut.

Laurie and I kicked into gear, filling out applications to cross-country ski areas every Friday night after work. The rule was we had to complete and call ten of them before we could go out on a hike or to the local tavern. We had been at it awhile—we'd filled out more than fifty—when, sometime in November, Laurie got offered a job as a ski instructor and groomer at a destination lodge on the North Rim of the Grand Canyon. I still had been offered nothing. Rejection from Cornell is one thing. Rejection from forty-nine lousy minimum-wage ski areas? I was starting to get depressed when the phone rang before dawn on a Saturday morning.

The energetic woman on the line launched into a long explanation about an employee who had stolen a few hundred dollars from the till and headed to Las Vegas. Not once, but twice. "We trusted him," she explained. "We really did."

"I believe you," I said earnestly. Then there was an awkward silence. "Who are you?"

"This is Joy," she said.

Joy was, it turned out, the owner of the North Rim lodge. The fellow who had stolen the till had been working at the front desk—checking guests in, answering phones, serving wine and beer, tasks I was pretty sure I could handle. Joy offered me the job right then, sight unseen—a practice that explained her problems with that other fellow, and one she would regret again after hiring me.

In the meantime, it seemed like destiny, like it was meant to be. I pictured an exclusive place where guests paid exorbitant prices (they did) and where the food was gourmet (it was) and where the setting was unspeakably beautiful (it was). I bought two sets of new clothes and a pair of shoes. I got a haircut. Then we saw the real thing.

❧

The lodge had been a summer-only establishment until the year before and was clearly not designed for winter at nine thousand feet. Shabby, it seemed, and ever on the brink of disaster. Pipes froze daily, and the maintenance staff hacked at the frozen earth with pickaxes. Snow blew in through the cracks in the walls of the cabin where we were assigned to sleep, drifting onto our pillows while we slept. We were not allowed to eat the gourmet food, only the special employee dish—frozen Stouffer's lasagna, usually, night after night. Then there was the water situation. Because the lodge sat on the high Kaibab plateau of impermeable limestone, there was no reliable water source. In summer, the owners trucked water in. Winter was trickier. Before the season began, they trucked in all the water they could store. After that, since vehicles could not reach the place (all guests arrived by snow cat, a two-hour journey) they relied on conservation methods. The high-paying guests were to conserve a little, and the low-paid staff members were to conserve a lot. We had no running water in our cabins, and we were allowed only one shower a week in a communal trailer filthy from overuse, so the staff, all of us, wore stocking caps even indoors to hide our greasy hair and layers of polarfleece to mask our stench. And instead of toilets, we used porta-potties, plastic cubitainers seasoned with unnamed blue chemicals, that could hold five gallons of human waste.

For two weeks Laurie and I worked long hours preparing the lodge to open over Christmas, slept fitfully in the frigid cabin, nursed stubborn colds, and tried to hide our disgruntlement. The other employees, younger than us and from the opposite edge of the continent, were laid back and patient, hanging on in hopes of one day working for Joy's other business, a Colorado river-rafting company. They ridiculed the place freely, calling themselves "Kaibab Trash" proudly, as if it were an exclusive club. A few of them had worked at the lodge the previous summer and showed off the sheet of notebook paper pinned to a linen-closet wall that listed everyone Joy had ever hired and how long they had lasted. Some were not even listed by name since they hadn't stayed that long. Gun Collector Dude: 7 hours. The Guy the Sheriff Came For: 2 hours. The Kaibab Trash laid back their heads and laughed. They maintained unflagging high spirits. They sat happily smoking American Spirit cigarettes and drinking microwaved instant coffee in the cavernous lodge when we were given frequent short breaks, while the nervous new manager—a man who'd come to the North Rim from Las Vegas where, he told us, it was tough to find a job in hospitality—stepped outside to smoke a joint, while I tried to gauge whether there was enough time to change out of my fancy new clothes and go for a ski.

Skiing, after all, was the main reason Laurie and I had come, and I figured I knew a little about it. I'd cross-country skied every winter in the Northwest, plodding up logging roads in leather ankle-high boots and on skis with metal edges. Back home, my friends told me these skis, classic Fischer E99s, were all wrong: far too lightweight, too skinny and with too much camber for carving turns around stumps in clearcuts. On the Rim, my skis were too heavy. The rental skis were narrow as yardsticks, made for the groomed track, and the boots were sleek Star Trek-looking slippers in bright Disney colors—pink, yellow, blue. For a long time, I'd have none of it. Wasn't the sport called "cross-country" not "in the track"? I'd skied on my E99s for years and, by god I was going to ski on them here. I skied daily, as far as I could during the breaks, acquiring blisters along the way, acclimating to the dizzying nine-thousand-foot altitude, proving myself.

But my complaints were nothing compared with Laurie's. She was working fourteen hours relearning how to ski in the Star Trek getup by day and learning to drive the enormous grooming machine by night. She was sick and exhausted, and on Christmas Eve she arrived home at 2:00 a.m. We opened gifts from our families, sipped from an expensive bottle of Scotch we'd picked up in Vegas, cried with self-pity and fell asleep.

By the day after Christmas, the situation called for heroics. I went to the young woman, Michele, who shared the front desk shift with me. The main lobby of the lodge featured a huge stone fireplace that gave off almost no heat, but did offer some ambiance at the price of several three-foot long-logs hourly. Every time I added one to the fire, a male guest would rise to offer me a hand.

"Awfully big job for a little girl like you," he'd say. Or something like that.

Michele was tossing logs on the fire when I entered.

"Hey," I said. "Where do you dump the porta-potties?"

"Don't even try it alone. It's a two-person job," she said.

I was thinking: I don't smoke cigarettes, I sleep in a forty-degree room. I was thinking: a two-person job, I'll be the judge of that.

"Well, where is it?" I asked.

"It's that big tank out back. You have to climb a ladder," she said.

I went out the back door where an oversized Swix ski wax thermometer displayed the temperature somewhere around zero. I looked up at a cylindrical tank with a narrow thirty-foot ladder going straight up its side. It did not look impossible to climb up there hauling forty pounds, but it didn't look easy either. I turned and went back into the lobby.

"The big tank with the ladder?"

The housekeepers were taking a break in the big stuffed chairs around the fireplace. A young man with soft whiskers curling about his chin and a battered Sears guitar slung on a rope around his neck, nodded empathetically.

"Totally," he said. "It totally sucks."

"Don't do it yourself," Michele said.

I stepped back outside and stared at the tank, marveling at how very much it must hold, how much human waste could be generated in one winter, and how the housekeeping staff—these people who apparently did not have the strength to climb out of their armchairs—could climb up there daily hauling porta-potties from twenty guest cabins. I felt humiliated, challenged. If they could do it, I figured, I should be able to.

So, I went back to our cabin and retrieved a porta-potty. The plastic box sported a convenient handle like a suitcase, and I felt silly carrying it out into the snow bundled as I was in a down coat and wool pants and ski boots with gaiters, like an airport traveler who took a wrong turn and ended up at the North Pole. I approached the ladder. The metal was too cold for me to take off my mittens, so I pawed the icy rungs awkwardly. I took the first step, pulling myself up with one hand, hauling the potty with the other. I leaned forward, my nose nearly touching the tank through the rungs of the ladder, so as not to fall backwards, and then I let go for the split second required to grope straight upwards for the next rung. Then I regained my balance and did it again. Only thirty rungs to go. I chastised myself for being so out of shape, for being so damned small, for ever bringing myself to this place, for misjudging those housekeepers who, it was clear now, were not lazy but constantly exhausted. I took another step. I was pretty sure I wasn't going to make it.

❧

It wasn't just me who misjudged the lodge. The brochure showed a skier on the postcard-perfect edge of the Grand Canyon, all red-orange spectacle and drama, as if such a view were out the front door. In fact, to see that view you would have to sign up for an additional overnight snowcat tour to a tiny backcountry hut, the size of a walk-in closet, that you'd share with other six other guests and a very smelly guide. The tour cost additional money, and along the way, though the brochure and the guides failed to mention the fact, the snowcat often overheated and stalled.

Guests didn't fuss about truth-in-advertising, though, I suppose because the actual setting distracted them. The lodge nestled in a patch of conifers in the center of a five-mile-long swath of meadow, slightly concave, like a very shallow dish or a serving platter, and was bordered on either side by trees—fºir, spruce, bare-trunked aspen (nearly all of it bark-carved, the most original reading in backwards mirror writing: Help! I'm stuck inside!). Across the meadow rose one gentle hill on which we practiced telemark turns on the yardstick skis during cloud-swirled sunsets, then skied home, turning occasionally to watch the sun trace elaborate shadows along our tracks. In the morning the sun rose brilliant, eye-smarting as we stepped out on snow that squeaked like Styrofoam under our skis. I had read a nineteenth-century novel about the Rocky Mountains shortly before arriving, where the narrator insisted that the "rarefied" high-elevation air was healing. I liked to ridicule the antiquated word "rarefied" both when I read the book and at the North Rim. In hindsight, I can see that it fit.

There was one view of the Grand Canyon that could be reached on skis in a mere four and a half miles. The view from the skiable viewpoint, the East Rim, was surprisingly subtle—not the deep red gashes and pillars you expect, but a longer, flatter view, far across the desert into which the Colorado starts to carve Marble Canyon, the earliest easternmost finger of the Grand. After a few weeks, when I'd finally beat the virus and abandoned the snivel and converted to the speedy rental skis, I skied there alone almost daily, learning to appreciate the nuances of light at different times of day, coming to terms with an entirely different Grand Canyon. More squiggle than gorge. It was the beginning.

✦

Loyalty does not come easily to me, to people, to places, even to skis. At the North Rim, I was reading Annie Dillard's *The Living*, a history of the early settlers in the Pacific Northwest, a book that made me homesick and steadfast. I spent my days behind the front desk playing cribbage with less-athletic guests and spouting about the Northwest tirelessly, tiresomely, to anyone who would listen. It's a graceless habit, vaunting one pretty place when you live in another, and I've learned to distrust it when I see it in others because after that winter on the Rim I know what it means: you are feeling seduced, and you are resisting.

✦

Twenty minutes I spent on that ladder, climbing with one arm. On the very last rung, my arm shaking with weakness, I believed I was going to have to drop the whole plastic contraption thirty feet to earth. I gathered my strength and flung the potty, instead, over the lip of the tank beside a manhole opening, the top of which appeared frozen over. I pulled the lever and, triumphant in my success, splattered the contents down the hatch. I climbed down easily and changed clothes for my shift in the lobby.

When Laurie got home sometime after midnight, I told her my story.

"Wow!" she said. Then she fell asleep.

A day passed, and Laurie returned home from work late again.

"Hey," she said. "George said he emptied his porta-potty and that it wasn't hard at all."

I thought about broad-shouldered ski instructor George, strong unflappable George, who looked like a wrestler and skied like an Olympian.

"That figures," I said.

The next day I saw the housekeepers heading out with a snowmobile trailer loaded with porta-potties ready to dump. How do they manage? I wondered. I watched them pull away from the lodge toward the classier, better-insulated guest cabins in the back.

"Where are you going?" I hollered.

Another bearded young man, with a passion for Phish and a bottomless capacity for humor, cut the engine and grinned.

"Where did you go?" he asked.

☙

It was the little things that, over time, began to outweigh the misery. Breakfast, for one thing, was made to order. I worked the early shift and wolfed down plates of fried potatoes drenched in veggies and cheese. And the gourmet lunch buffet was open to employees, a free-for-all of cold cuts and fruit salads and a scrumptious pumpkin soup. What is the secret ingredient? I asked the chef, and he showed me crates of whole cream that crowded the walk-in. Consume calories per day equal to the elevation where you live, the chef recommended. I suspect we came close.

The guests, when they arrived, were pleasant and undemanding. Many had won weekend getaways in radio contests or had finagled free passes from Joy, who was a strong believer in word-of-mouth advertising. Some had scrimped their savings, their pensions, and they arrived in wool knickers and sweaters, endearing themselves to us, making my old-fashioned gear look shiny and newfangled. They took ski lessons gamely—what else was there to do?—and rarely complained about the water or even the porta-potties. One weekend the visitor list included the name James Taylor. The real James Taylor! The staff, the women especially, went wacky, starstruck. My knees went weak. And even though he claimed a thumb injury that kept him from playing his guitar for us (we were pretty sure he was faking), even he was kind and humble.

Midweek, when the guests were gone, the lodge became another place entirely, a little *Shining*esque in its remoteness, but cozy nevertheless and rich with the camaraderie of a bunch of neighborhood kids camping in a secret fort. We huddled by the fireplace and played late-night games of Scrabble. Nate, the guitar player, worked out Dylan tunes on the Sears guitar. The nylon strings reverberated dully, and in the undersized body the chords echoed flatly like a ukulele, and he imitated Dylan's whine, and there was not a better guitar anywhere to fit the scene. We were glad, secretly I think, that James Taylor never played there. It wouldn't have been the same.

So it was that the place, like the frost-coated pom-poms of Ponderosa needles reflecting sunlight at dawn, for a short time began to take on an unlikely, almost magical sheen.

❧

There was silence for a moment before I set off at a dead sprint toward the machine grooming the lesson lanes in front of the main lodge.

"Pack!" I cried to Laurie.

"What?"

I signaled with a frantic finger across my own neck for her to cut the engine.

"We gotta get out of here," I said.

"What?"

No time to mince words. "I dumped it in the water."

Laurie looked confused.

"The porta-potty," I said. She looked at me in horror.

It was a look I'd get used to. The other employees were savvy and loyal; they laughed good-naturedly and were not about to tell, my first clue that these were the kind of people to keep in the clutch of friendship. Laurie was not going to tell. At that point, I think, she preferred to pack and bail.

The buck stopped with me and with my Catholic conscience.

"I dumped my porta-potty in the water," I told the manager. What else was there to say?

He stared at me heavy lidded.

"Did you hear me?"

He dialed the telephone and handed it to me. "Joy," he said.

I told her the whole unsavory story.

"Oh, thank you! Thank you!" Joy gushed, and I was confused, imagining an insurance scam or an early season cut-the-losses shutdown.

"Thank you for telling me," she exclaimed. "I've never had an employee who would tell something like that."

Joy contacted the proper authorities, or claimed to, and determined that the problem, apparently, stemmed not so much from the waste, which would be neutralized by the chlorine added to the water at regular intervals, but from those unnamed blue chemicals. The answer would be to ship in drinking water via snowcat for the rest of the winter and, the housekeepers joked, to keep our lips sealed tight during our weekly showers. Meanwhile, two young maintenance workers were sent to the top of the tank to chip away with pickaxes at my frozen mess.

While the public health details were being sorted out, I worked my shift behind the front desk. Since it was holiday season and some festivities had been planned, guests wanted to know why they could not shower.

"I don't know." I shrugged. "One of those maintenance things."

I went to throw another log on the fire.

"Let me help you with that." A middle-aged skier struggled out of a stuffed chair. "It's almost as big as you are."

If he'd only known. If he'd only asked anyone at that lodge, they'd have told him that, despite my size, strength is not my shortcoming.

She's strong all right, they'd have said. But she's not real smart.

☙

In the early days of March, bare patches of dry ground began to widen at an alarming rate, not even melting at that latitude and altitude, but *transpiring*—a new distinctly unNorthwestern word—transforming directly from solid to gas. It was liberating to think of all that snow and no mud whatsoever, like sin without penance. Soon many of the other employees would go straight to the Colorado to work on Joy's river-raft trips, the glorious Southwestern ski bum/river rat routine. We basked in the sun midweek, the snowmobiles circled up like wagons, the cats people had somehow been hiding in their cabins out prowling out onto the crust, sniffing the air.

On the last weekend an energetic group of ski instructors from Vail arrived for a workshop, and Laurie drove them in, letting them ski behind the snow van on long ropes, cranking themselves from side to side, cutting sharp telemark turns like water-skiers until the transmission began to smoke, and on the very last night, everyone—guests, employees, Vail guys—skied out to the East Rim viewpoint to watch the sun set and the moon rise simultaneously over the desert. There was a bonfire and chocolate fondue, something with a few thousand calories, and a fast cold ski back to the lodge under the dome of a bazillion stars, bright still, always, despite the moonlight. Afterwards, when the guests retreated to their cabins, we sat around the fireplace. The Vail guys played covers of Little Feat and the Allman Brothers on the rope-slung guitar. Nate played Dylan. I even took a turn, though I rarely played in public—the Grateful Dead, the Beatles, James Taylor even. What the hell? A game of hacky sak ensued, played with potted plastic plants, and players with plastic violets stuck behind their ears climbed onto the log beams overhead for impromptu gymnastics. Shortly before dawn, Michele drew back her arm in a mighty pitcher's windup and chucked an empty gin bottle into the fireplace, and the crowd cheered. When I returned a couple hours later to restart the fire for my last morning shift, there were no shards of glass in the fireplace at all, no remnant of what had been there only a short time before.

The staff cleaned the lodge that day and gathered for the final porta-potty brigade of the winter. The tank, it turned out, was a dinky affair with a ten-rung ladder leaning at a gentle angle against it, but it was still too unpleasant a job to face alone. In the middle of it, the manager stepped out to tell me Joy was on the phone. She wanted to speak with me. A family emergency? I worried. Or a demand for reparations taken from my meager paycheck? I tromped toward the lodge in snowboots and shorts, and picked up the receiver.

"Hello?"

"I wondered if you and Laurie would like to work on the river this summer," Joy said.

The river! They would be minimum-wage jobs, I knew, with hellacious work schedules, but on the Colorado River!

"Let me call you back," I said.

Laurie and I skied away to contemplate our options. It would mean starting over, trading logging boots for sandals, hand tools for oars, solitude for servitude. It would mean glorious hot sun and cold cold water and more unexplored settings of unspeakable beauty. It was sorely tempting. We sat in silence in the sun-soaked meadow. I pictured hanging glaciers and towering firs and wildflowers—trillium and bunchberry and Queen's cup—that by now would be appearing in the valleys back home and would trail the retreating snow, higher and higher, through the summer. I looked at Laurie, and I knew I didn't have to explain. Our loyalties, despite everything, remained steadfast and a thousand miles away.

We left the rim, left the state. We overloaded our Toyota so much that we blew out the transmission driving over Death Valley. When we faced the polyester-clad salesman at Aamco, I argued fiercely.

"You can't blow a manual transmission."

Well, we had, and we spent every penny that was left of the winter's wages to replace it, though it never did work right again.

Back in the Northwest, spring flowers straggled a few weeks behind my imagination, the first tiny yellow glacier lilies barely poking their way through the slush. I headed out for trail work in a rainstorm slipping and stumbling in the ankle-twisting mud. The crew tensions from last fall had not abated, and by the time we stopped for lunch, eating standing up, hopping from one foot to the other to stay warm, no one was speaking. Maybe it had been a mistake to return. Maybe it had been a mistake to go, to be seduced by all that sunshine. What, after all, did I have to show for the whole grueling exhilarating experience?

"Well, I've got a story," I said.

Entombing Spiders and Other Small Shack Stories

*It's the end of an era, I suppose. No more of the seasonal housing merry-*go-round that has spun us from house to house, seventeen of them in half as many years. A wild hair at a wild party inspired us to throw our savings together with friends—a married couple, seasonals like us, former hotshot firefighters—and make a bid on a piece of land that none of us thought we could afford. Some months of complicated real-estate negotiations followed that we feared, and sometimes hoped, would come to nothing. Then on Friday, February 13, via fax machine from Arizona, we closed the deal. Now we are landed gentry. Dirt poor. Home.

These five acres that we'll eventually subdivide have two existing structures: a smallish house (about seven hundred square feet) that most recently housed a family of seven, and a tiny sleeping cabin that we call "the shack." For a bunch of mutually agreed-upon reasons, our land partners, Tony and Loretta, moved into the house. Laurie and I have the shack. The shack, it turns out, is of the same dimensions as both Henry David Thoreau's idyllic retreat along Walden Pond and the convicted Unabomber's shack in Montana. So, we're wondering this: Are we living simply? Or are we crazy as heck?

We moved in last March, and we promptly invited friends to the first party on Friday, March 13. We left the woodstove heating the place while, feeling lucky as can be, we gathered with friends around a barbecue in the snow. When we returned inside, exhausted and ready for sleep, Laurie faced her worst nightmare. Laurie is plenty brave. Except when it comes to arachnids. That night spiders poured through every crack and pinhole into the newfound warmth. Hundreds of them. The continuous parade, every shape and variety imaginable, was enough even to unnerve me, and I don't mind spiders a bit. Laurie poured a full mug of red wine and fished out a thick roll of green duct tape. She stayed up half the night taping over every conceivable entry way. "Entombing them," she explained with obvious glee. The parade slowed, then hours later, finally stopped. We survived. Laurie even slept. The duct tape made an interesting decorative touch.

Snow melted early. Glacier lilies, then trillium, blanketed the yard. Birds sang unceasingly, beautifully, through the day. We worked hard at our regular jobs all week. We worked twice as hard, if twice as slowly, at home on the weekends. Built a bed, a table, shelves, and whatever the thing is called that holds the sink basin. We cut a new window into the back wall, not exactly square, but airy nonetheless. As the snow uncovered piles of discarded treasures in the yard, Tony and I piled them into the truck to haul off to the local garbage dump. Later, Laurie would return from the dump with the very same treasures. If not Laurie, then Loretta.

Early in the spring, two mysterious rusty cones began to protrude from the melting snow. Trying to stick to my self-imposed rule that I would not throw out anything if I did not know what it was, I ignored them. Finally, I raised my courage to ask Tony what he thought they might be. He cleared his throat. "A reclining goddess?" he guessed. With that, we wrestled them onto the truck and hauled them off. Later we learned that the cones were historic warming stoves used by the loggers who had cleared the head of the Lake Chelan early in the twentieth century. Neighbors heard the story and, luckily, hurried to the dump to rescue history.

Meanwhile, I spent a number of Saturdays with a shovel and rock bar in search of water. We knew there was a water line somewhere in front of the shack that went from the well house to Tony and Loretta's house, we just didn't know exactly where. I called it "adventure digging," and soon I had a pit nearly as deep as a gravesite that made negotiating the way to the outhouse especially difficult. Eventually, I found the pipe and, with Loretta's help, plumbed cold water into the shack. Nothing about those first few weeks seemed simple.

I've read *Walden* more than once. I studied it some in college. I debated it repeatedly with ski bum friends in taverns. Don't get me wrong. I respect Thoreau's experiment with living simply with nature. But the way I understand it, H. David lived only two miles out of town where his friends, the Emersons, always had a warm meal and company awaiting him. Though he fails to mention it, I imagine Thoreau's friends were also there to assist with the less philosophical problems of life: hauling wood and water, getting supplies, making repairs. Simple living, I've come to believe, requires a certain amount of freeloading. So far this year, Laurie and I have been given a woodstove, a microwave, a dresser, a kitchen sink, cabinets, rosebushes, cedar trees, and jalapeño plants. We've been loaned more tools than I could name. We've begged advice on plumbing, construction, gardening. Forget living simply. We have our neighbors to thank for the fact that we are simply living.

Besides, I'm not sure that H. David, or the Unabomber for that matter, would approve of our lean-to full of material possessions. Four bikes. Six pair of skis. Rice cooker. Pepper grinder. Ziploc bags of miscellaneous photos. Enough holey and mismatched wool socks to chink a log house. On and on. We've dragged the stuff around for years, from home to home to home, in search of this, its (hopefully) final destination. Now there's the microwave, an early '80s model that takes two of us to lift and sports as much chrome as a Chevrolet bumper. There's the fairly necessary Husqvarna chainsaw and the extremely necessary electric fan. There's the outdoor fridge wrapped in tire chains for bear protection and the single-burner hot plate, a gift from Laurie's grandma in North Dakota. There's a five-disc CD player, a large FM antenna, and yes, well, this laptop computer. You get the picture. Doing without, we ain't.

That leaves the other option. Crazy? Lawyers paid to ship the Unabomber's shack from Montana to California as evidence of his mental imbalance. So, although Laurie and I aren't inclined to build bombs just yet, occasionally family members will ask gingerly: "Are you *sure* you haven't made a mistake?" They mean the cabin and the isolation. They mean the complicated land partnership, and of course, the money. Was it a mistake to go into debt for a spidery shack six miles from a boat landing, fifty-five miles from a grocery store, many years from Internet access?

Well, it's another brilliant sunny morning, and there's more work to do. We've decided that, after all, we need a little more space. We're gonna build a tiny addition out back. Truth is, I don't know a thing about construction. Ditto for Laurie. So we're in for some frustration, I'm afraid. That, and plenty of dust from the buses passing on the road. But this afternoon, after the dust settles and the downlake breeze moves in, I'm gonna be sitting at the picnic table out back, watching the sprinkler in the garden, swatting mosquitoes. Relaxing at home. Will I be *sure* then that I haven't made a mistake? Yep. Crazy, maybe. But *sure*, for sure.

To the Woods

❧

I'm standing on the high ground of our property—the Bench, we call it.
The Bench, so far, remains undeveloped, pristine, thickly forested
with fir, pine, dogwood, maple. From here, I can look across the
steep U-shaped valley toward ridges dusted with first snow and
down to a meandering river fed by creeks that plummet from alpine
meadows.

The low ground, where Laurie and I live, is a little less
glamorous. The cabin has four insulated walls, three windows, a
woodstove, cold water, and electricity. It does not have hot water,
a telephone, or a toilet. When I describe this to people, I face either
admiration or disdain. One friend, a high school teacher who has a
thing for *Walden*, thinks this is a neat philosophical exercise. Every
year he crowds his students into a masking-tape square the exact
dimensions of Thoreau's cabin (and roughly those of ours) while
he waxes poetic. Other friends—older friends, mostly, who have
our own interest at heart, I know—point out that this way of life is
over-idealized, out of date, and physically impossible to sustain
past a certain age.

As for Thoreau, I don't have much patience for woodsy
righteousness. As for the hardships, I don't need reminding. There
is wood to split, plumbing to insulate, snow to shovel in winter, a
garden to maintain in summer. This lifestyle, I want to tell my
schoolteacher friend, is anything but simple. The upside is that it's
temporary.

We plan to build something new. For our own comfort, sure.
Mostly, we plan to build on higher ground because our little shack
sits smack in the middle of the floodplain. Last month the river

came charging through our vegetable garden three feet deep and surrounded our cabin entirely. With spring meltoff looming on the horizon, we are a little eager to get moving.

That's why we're on the Bench. Today we have to choose which trees to cut in order to install a septic system. Light snow is falling, and it is becoming increasingly clear—as it did when we built our driveway and will again, surely, when we build the house—that more trees than we thought will have to come down. We'll fall them ourselves, then a neighbor will mill them into fine clear boards. But the utilitarian excuses don't do much to ease my conscience. Developer. I roll the ugly word over my tongue trying to make it stick.

Of course, I'm not the only one. We have at least a half dozen friends doing exactly the same thing, and most of them have been at it longer. They came to the woods like we did, lured by seasonal work; they fell in love with one place and stayed ten, twenty, thirty years. They bought a little piece of undeveloped land because that's what they could afford, and they built a little shack smaller than the limit above which a building permit is required. They work for wages through the summer, then work by hand through the winter on insurmountable tasks. One friend in his fifties has terraced his steeply forested five-acre lot by hand—shovel by shovel, rock by rock—building retaining walls, pushing a wheelbarrow, and in his spare time, building storage sheds, planting rye and vetch as cover crops in his garden.

Most of these friends are bitter about the thick clot of hoops that would-be developers have to jump, and I'm pretty sympathetic. I spend about three hours a week standing in line at the one pay phone in the valley trying to get straight answers from the county. What? I say. I already paid that. Oh, those were the application fees and the review fees; these are the filing fees. Got it. I remind myself that our complaint—that the rules are unreasonably complicated—is minor compared to the alternative. We are one step away from being unable to live out here at all.

Land prices here in second-home paradise rival those in downtown Seattle, and jobs are hard to come by, most often seasonal with little hope of advancement. ("Career," as C. J. Rawlins once quipped, "rhymes with beer out here.") Anti-growth laws are the icing on the cake. Minimum lot size and zoning codes keep even shack ownership out of reach for most of our peers. To choose to live in the woods (to become "downwardly mobile" as one friend who works on Wall Street coined it) becomes less an option by the day. Maybe we need to accept that fact and its logical consequence: move to Portland or Seattle, or Medford or Wenatchee for that matter. Maybe we need to find office jobs and save up for a mortgage on a place with a short commute. Save the woods for the weekends.

That's the environmentally correct answer, I know. David Quammen ends his exhaustive study of shrinking biodiversity *Song of the Dodo* with a plea to would-be Thoreaus: Don't do it. Don't move out there. Don't develop anymore. That's what a lot of people believe. I can see it in their eyes: You are in your thirties. You are college educated. Be done with this. You do not belong.

After three years of entanglement with the county planning department, that's what I've decided it all comes down to: who belongs. If space is limited—and it is, rightly—who should get it? Surely not the third- and fourth-home owners that I overhear making real-estate deals on their cell phones in trendy small-town cafes. That, maybe, we can all agree on. The other alternative, the underlying foundation of the most convoluted bureaucratic regulations and the most elegantly crafted intellectual arguments, is this: locals only. That was the attitude of Tom McCall's Oregon, the residue of which I faced when I first arrived the Northwest, in Eugene, awestruck by the beauty.

These days, "community" is the buzz word, and rural folks in the Northwest have learned to throw it around like a tonic, like a defense. We must maintain our communities. Keep jobs in the community. It's an appealing word, an appealing idea. Everywhere

I go, I meet unsettled thirtysomething community seekers. Sometimes the urban emigrants get annoyingly hung up on last best place details—wanting a good bakery, a small ski area, maybe an airport within a reasonable distance—but their desire to belong somewhere smaller than a Greater Metropolitan Area is genuine. They come to the Northwest, to the woods, hoards of them, looking for home, and they—we!—make all the community talk a bit more complicated.

Who exactly is the community, and when do you become a member? After how many generations? Or up here, where wet snow can pile fifteen feet high, after how many winters? At what point can you bury the fact that you drove west in the sixties and traded your VW van for a can of Copenhagen and a Stihl ball cap? Or that you left southern California halfway through the Reagan Administration, hanging on trees as a lifeline? The big question is who gets to decide, and the ironic answer for those of us who came from elsewhere, or whose ancestors did, is that we do. We decide.

Often I read that the big question facing the Northwest is what we want the landscape to look like in twenty or fifty years. It's also, whether we want to admit it or not, who we want to be here in twenty or fifty years. The right answer, the only good answer, is: whoever wants to. That's what the free marketers say, too, and if we agree, then it's fair game for those cell-phone developers who, when I overhear them, make me want to start a revolution. It's a vicious circle and it gives me a headache, frankly, but it's an important question—maybe *the* important question—and the one I read about least, maybe because it necessarily becomes so personal. Do I belong? Why or why not? How do I make myself belong?

Back on the Bench, it's clear that a few big trees—trees! trees! what I came here for in the first place!—will have to go. Don't get me wrong. I cut trees all the time at work without a thought, knowing there are so many more out there, unhealthy numbers of them, and that others will grow back in the blink of an eye. This sheepishness is something altogether new, a heavy cloak of responsibility to go with my scratchy new owner/builder garb. Despite my natural skepticism toward all things New Age, I'm having trouble resisting the urge to apologize to them, to explain that the ones that are left will get more sunlight, more nutrients, and that we will plant new ones. I want to pretend that the trees understand. Getting people to understand, that's the kicker. We love it here. We want to be here. It's the back-to-nature bit, sure, and maybe we are twenty-five or a hundred and fifty years too late, but we are going to stay, not because of tired nostalgia or youthful idealism, not because we own the land, but because the land owns us. In the long run, that might be the only definition of belonging that matters.

Red Tape and Yellow Stickies

When I started building a house in a tiny remote corner of nowhere, I suspected some challenges, but red tape wasn't one of them. I'd heard warnings about red tape, how it entangles bureaucracy like the blackberry vines that try to choke our garden. But I pretty much ignored them. I don't like stereotypes, especially ones about the government, since I'm a fed myself. Then, a couple years ago, I started the process of obtaining permits (building, water, septic) from the county. In the end, it wasn't red tape that got to me. It was one yellow post-it note.

I was convinced in the beginning that as long as I followed every rule to the letter, these county permits would, if not fly through, at least plod along. They didn't. Over a year passed while one application, in particular, sat in the wrong file or got sent to the wrong office, then seemingly disappeared entirely. One morning I called from the one outdoor satellite phone we share in this valley, and I spent twenty wintery minutes on hold while the receptionist searched for my file.

"What was the application year on that one again?" she asked when she finally returned.

"1999."

"Oh," she said, "you should have told me it's from 1999."

"Well," I said, "it's from 1999." I felt hopeful, having cleared that up, like maybe we were getting somewhere.

"Because 1992 thru 1999 are missing right now."

"Right now today, or right now for the rest of the week, or what?"

"Just right now."

I decided to switch gears from patient martyr to amateur sleuth. Call different county offices at different times. Call and hang up until I got a new receptionist. At last I figured out where the lost application might be. I wrote to that office (having lost some faith in the phone) and sure enough, they replied that they had the application on file. However, they explained, one necessary document was missing. I knew the document well. Three months prior I'd taken a special trip to the county seat to hand deliver it.

I got on the phone right away.

"You hand delivered it? Then it's at the auditor's office."

"Right. The county auditor's office."

"But we don't have it here."

"Can you go get it?"

"No," she said. "You'll have to do that."

I explained that I live in a very remote area and work full-time, and that I had, in fact, already taken one special trip to deliver this very same piece of paper. Was there any other possibility?

"Hmm," she said. "You could have them fax it to us." Geez, couldn't *she* have them fax it to her? I couldn't be too choosy.

"OK, can you transfer me to that office?"

"No, I am sorry," she said, eternally polite. "Good luck." She hung up.

I looked up the number for the auditor's office, waited for the satellite connection, and dialed the thirty-five numbers required to make another calling-card call. When I got through, I explained the situation to the next receptionist.

"So, can you fax that document?"

"Yes, but it will cost one dollar."

"Fine, fine," I said. What's another dollar?

She paused. "Paid in advance."

"Do you mean …" I reined in hard on my anger, tried to put on my cheeriest gritted-teeth voice, "… that I have to send you a dollar before you will fax this document to an office across the street?"

"Yes," she said.

1:15 p.m. Mail goes out of this valley at 1:30 only three times a week by boat. I'd have to hustle to jump-start this application before it got lost again. (*We're sorry*, they might say, *but the letter S is missing right now*.) I rifled through the car ashtray and found three crumpled bills, enough to buy a pre-stamped envelope and to include an extra dollar for good measure.

I sprinted up the post office steps, scribbled a note with every possible name, number, or filing code under which the document might be found (or lost), folded cash into the envelope, and sent off my request.

A week passed. I told a few people about my exasperation with red tape, and eventually, when I calmed down, I felt ashamed. It isn't the county's fault I live in the backwoods, I told myself. I can't expect special treatment. Besides, I reasoned, this is probably an oddity, a bad day (or string of them, perhaps), entirely out of the ordinary. I thought of all the times hikers have passed me on the trail while I'm eating lunch, off the clock, and how they probably thought to themselves: Ha! Lazy government worker wasting tax dollars. Stereotypes, I reminded myself, are just no good.

Finally, a letter arrived postmarked from the county. Approval, I thought, feeling victorious, and virtuous, too. I had waded patiently through the muck—or mostly patiently—and now here was my reward. Of course, the envelope weighed a little less than I might have expected, but what's there to say? *You're good to go. All set. Thanks for the many fees you have paid.* I tore it open and out flew the hand-scrawled note I had written to them a week before, with one yellow post-it note affixed, the small size, with a polite and neatly printed message: *I'm sorry. We do not fax documents.* The crumpled dollars were nowhere to be found.

The Old Wagon Road

❧

Yesterday we scouted a new trail or, I should say, a sort of new one. We walked the remains of a wagon road that was built a hundred years ago or so by miners who forged deep into these mountains in search of copper and silver and gold, and which is now slated to be rebuilt as a trail for tourists who journey into the mountains in search of solace or splendor or distraction. The project is estimated to cost a few million dollars to complete, more than two hundred thousand just to plan, so whether it will ever be funded is anyone's guess. I'm pretty skeptical. I lack the imagination for envisioning progress in seven figures. Sometimes I lack the imagination for envisioning progress at all. Right now, for me, that's a problem.

❧

The old wagon road roughly parallels the existing valley road, and the grade is mostly intact except for short obliterated stretches at the base of steep avalanche chutes or rock slides. So our job was not particularly hard. We carried rolls of blue flagging instead of heavy tools, strolled rather than hiked, and it felt like a lark, like a coup, for three of us to be out on an early-season work day, skidding over patches of snow, watching our breath billow in the cool morning mist while Phil described his dental hygienist again, the one he says looks exactly like Cheryl Tiegs.

"Don't I look like Cheryl Tiegs?" I asked.

"You look like Danny DeVito," he said.

Even I had to laugh.

We flagged the route through an uncommonly open forest— firs and pines the diameter of fifty-five gallon drums, big for around here. A hundred yards to the south, on the other side of the road, the river churned with runoff; a hundred yards to the north, mountainsides rose clifflike, etched with the steep dusty trails where we'll work the rest of the summer. Something about this in-between spot felt disconcerting, liberating.

"Look," Jason said, "no brush."

He was right. There were no berry brambles, no vine maples, none of the rabid fecundity that usually clogs this second-growth forest. Humans had, apparently, meddled less right there, in recent years, than elsewhere in the valley, and trees had shot up unhindered and shaded out the understory, victorious. Of course, we knew that was likely to change if this project goes through. When we fall trees to build the new trail, sunlight will burn through the canopy and brush will take root. For now it seemed, well, pristine. Even though it used to be a road.

Such is the cycle I've learned working on trails. You scar up the earth, tear it to bits, to build a drainage diversion, say, or to widen tread. A year later, you can hardly tell where you've been: moss appears; leaves land and turn, by turns, into litter, duff, fertilizer, finally, for sedges and swordferns; in time trees sprout and shoot skyward for decades, then topple in windstorms; so we cut the logs, and the process starts over again. Nature recovers, then succumbs again. Just like we do. Spring arrives and drags me out of pseudo-hibernation with my clothes clean and my boots greased, happy to be back at it, carefree enough to shrug off teasing. Danny DeVito, no less! Then sometime in mid-August, when I am bone-weary and black fly-addled, I will swear off trails forever. I will announce that I am ready, finally, to retire and eat bonbons and watch soap operas. It happens every year, and no one dares tease me then. By October, they know, I will be back to my senses. It's a cycle we're accustomed to, rhythmic and predictable, a way of life that neither inflicts nor suffers much permanent damage. It's a cycle that I fear has left me ill prepared to tackle big projects, like rebuilding the wagon road, or more immediately, like building my own home.

In one section, the old wagon road passes behind the property where Laurie and I are in the early stages of building

"Getting ready to mill?" Jason asked as we flagged our way by.

"I guess," I said.

I glanced around at the trees we felled in winter, bucked into twenty-foot lengths, scattered pell-mell. It looked like the wreckage from a tornado.

"Rafters first, then joists," I said. "We'll buy the two by fours downtown."

I tried to say it with confidence, with hope, but I wasn't fooling anyone. Phil and Jason stopped by to lend a hand last week when I was digging a thirty-foot section of power ditch by hand in the rocky soil. River-rounded boulders wedged tight as elevator passengers did not yield readily, and the hours of digging bred fears like blisters. Turns out I'm scared to death of building this cabin. I'm afraid that I am being environmentally destructive or financially irresponsible, that I am too unskilled, that the cabin will never get done, or that when it does, it will burn down or be smashed by a falling tree. When Phil and Jason showed up, I was frantic to get my ditch to utility district specifications, afraid my electrical permit application would be refused.

"Still fretting, Danny?" Jason asked.

"Always," I said. "Without fail."

⟨❧

Beyond the cabin site, we clambered over a particularly nasty slide, five-hundred-pound rocks balanced precariously atop splintered tree trunks. It was a little dicey getting over, and we discussed how to blast through the section; we scribbled numbers in pocket notebooks, pounds of explosives needed, guesses really.

"Then, when we're done, it'll slide again," Phil said.

"Job security," I said.

We repeat this conversation at work weekly, sometimes daily, like a mantra. A lot of what we build on trails is temporary. Footlogs collapse under snow weight. Bridges tear off their footings in avalanches. Signs get chewed by bears. When it floods, the trails managers, our office bosses, hire helicopters to document damage before the rain even slows because disaster dollars are easier to come by than maintenance funds. Catastrophes keep me employed, I remind myself. Destruction is building my house. Uncertainty is part of the bargain.

That has suited me fine up until now. The future itself has always been, for me, an uncertain notion, rarely a question of *if* it will come crashing down but *how*: the feathery nuclear end descending like winter or pesticides mutating wildly, out of control, gnawing hungrily at my innards, at the earth's. The four horsemen ride in my blind spot, always approaching just out of view. To plan for the future is to tempt fate. Permanence a dangerous notion. Safer to cheer when the trail slides yet again. Safer to keep moving.

ໝ

The sun strained over the ridgetop, and we squinted in the unfamiliar brightness, shed our raincoats. We passed rocks piled beside the old wagon road at regular intervals, rocks the same size and shape as the ones I dug by hand at the cabin, placed there the same laborious way I did it: one at a very slow time. The difference, I thought, was this: twenty miles instead of thirty feet. When we reconstruct this trail the differences between us and the men who built it the first time around will be these: chainsaws, backhoes, helicopters, overtime pay. All these and more. If I think my life is hard, I oughta be ashamed of myself.

Written history in a place like this is a little sketchy. Journals of early travel writers abound, but they are long on adjectives, short on facts. I can find no fixed date when the wagon road was originally constructed. It probably evolved from the horse trail that accessed Bridge Creek, a mining settlement fifteen miles up the road that boasted its own post office around the turn of the century, but which is now a small campground. As good as the mining may have been, folks never stayed. The place was a little too remote, the weather a little too lousy. I've tried, occasionally, to find any sign of the attempted settlement—a cabin foundation or a crumbling stone hearth. I've had no luck. The first automobile drove to Bridge Creek in 1914; the journal from that trip reports that except for a few stumps that needed to be removed, the road was in pretty good shape. The same report could stand today.

If I don't know specifically about the road, I know a little, anecdotally, about the white people who settled the area. They came from elsewhere, from everywhere, and finding the easy-access places pretty well saturated, they just kept moving, against insurmountable odds. One pregnant woman, so the story goes, rowed a boat with her husband fifty-five miles up the lake to start a homestead. Aspiring orchardists (Californians no less, like me, the bane of Northwesterners) moved in, and cut eight acres of forest by hand, then pulled the stumps to plant apple trees that still produce today. Packers hauled picks and shovels and explosives on mules along craggy ridges to the tops of granite peaks where they constructed fire lookouts, the crown jewels of the mountains, that were later destroyed when the 1964 Wilderness Act mandated the human-made out.

The sheer boldness of it—the achy mud-crusted hope it takes to build—seems so far from the idea of progress as I've known it, the one that rings of the Jetsons, of the Internet, of people in very fashionable clean clothes or spacesuits, of gadgets with buzzers: cell phones, palm pilots, car alarms. The newest thing is always shinier and shoddier than the one before, and I feel myself cluttered by the stuff of it. CDs sound better, they told us, and never break. The newer mountain bike is faster and lighter, the shocks easier on the joints. The new car is sleeker, and safer in a collision. And computers! Before spring flowers fade, the computer I'm typing on will become obsolete and there will be a new one that I'll need, and the old one, mine and everyone else's, will jam up the landfill, and it starts all over. There's the materialism that bristles, the real space it all takes up, then there's the mind space it gobbles too, the brainpower it takes to stay on top of what's new and better. It's exhausting and suffocating, and it makes me insensibly mad. I don't want to deal with it, any of it, and if I'm shirking my role in society, in the development of civilization, or at least the upkeep of the domestic economy, so be it. Call it nostalgia or escapism or Peter Pan pretend: I'd rather work out here in the woods chopping logs and digging dirt.

∽

"The Mariners traded him in '97 to the Expos, I think."

The guys had moved on to talking baseball, a sign that the day was going smoothly, that spirits were running high. Baseball's their favorite subject, bar none, and one I haven't followed much since I was ten years old. I listened distractedly as usual and took part in what I could.

"You know that guy, Ana Maria?"

"Is he kind of a stocky duck-footed guy like the third baseman for the '79 Dodgers?"

This conversation will travel from here to November. Baseball's like a soap opera, I think, or like land-use politics; if you followed it continually for a few months in the '70s, you can follow the storyline now. Of course, the trick is never to bring up a well-known player like Ken Griffey Jr. or Johnny Bench. Everyone already has an opinion on them. The trick is to choose the almost forgotten players. There's more room to speculate, then, more to the story.

"No, no," Phil said. "He's more like Nettles. Remember? With the Yankees?"

"Sure. I remember."

The old wagon road began to climb, skirting the ankles of the mountains thirty feet above the valley floor. The slope was not stable enough to hold itself so we looked around for retaining walls, and there they were, mossy and lichened, sturdy and sure as ever— five, ten, fifteen feet high. The walls were built by hand, the same inexpert way that we build rock walls on trails, with larger rocks on the bottom, then, at a slight incline toward the tread, smaller and progressively less-well-shaped rocks, chinked with smaller triangular rocks, flyrock from blasting.

There's a secret thrill in this, in finding the scars of other people's work. I will be crouching in the brush on a trail that has been neglected, lopping and lopping, far beyond the clearing limits, farther than seems reasonable, farther, I'll be certain, than anyone has ever lopped before, when I'll find a willow stump, then another, then a whole row of stobs. Someone was here first! It feels like camaraderie, like maybe we share the same palm-calloused pleasures: smoothing over fresh-dug dirt and shaking saw chips from your socks, smelling the heady spice of needles, the head-hit smell of rock on rock. It's invigorating and addicting, the doing of it. When the early settlers came, it is hard to imagine that their first notion was progress, hard to believe they were envisioning posterity. That happens by accident, doesn't it? Or the best of it does?

"You think we can keep these walls like they are?" Phil asked.

"I hope so," I said, eyeing one rubbly section. "They might need some sprucing up."

In about three hours, we had reached the end of the short stretch of the wagon road we had been assigned to survey. We reemerged on the regular road, muddy and potholed this time of year, and tried to consolidate our notes.

"It's not much to brag about," Jason said in summation..

True enough. The high-country trails that switchback for miles up to three-sixty views of glaciated peaks then meander across velvety meadows, those trails are something to brag about. The wagon road won't ever be a spectacular trail, just a safer place to wander than on the existing one-lane road where bikers and hikers share the space with tour buses and the occasional dump truck. It will be a place apart, and god knows if people need anything in these progress-pressed days, they need places apart. The irony is that to make it a place apart, we are going to have to clear it and grade it and harden it and put up signs.

"Maybe we could just sort of leave it like it is," I suggested lamely.

We all know the answer to that: it's not ours to decide if things get constructed, just how. If the proposal doesn't go through, the funding dollars don't arrive, and we don't get paid, at least not until some new natural disaster comes along. It's tempting nonetheless to leave well enough alone.

"I don't know," Phil said. "Hikers will struggle at the rock slides, get lost and annoyed. There's liability to think about. And horses, well, you can forget about horses the way things look now. Be kinda silly to have a trail called the wagon road where horses can't even go."

Jason and I knew he was right, so we began to gather our observations and measurements and guesses into a plan, how best to change the place to keep it unchanged, how to maintain that woodsy cloistered feel so different from the show-offy elation offered higher up in the mountains where trails slash z's across sidehills as they climb, where if you're hiking, you can be spotted from miles away. It can be a modest trail, maybe, and my cabin can be a modest home. It's OK to build, I tried to persuade myself. It doesn't always have to be a cliché, the expected, Nolan Ryan form of progress. We stood in the road-cut swath of unseasonable sunlight, and sipped tea from our thermoses, and it was a relief, in a way, to leave the past behind, to speculate about possibilities, about the prospects for the season ahead.

"It could be our year," Phil said.

I didn't know if he meant us or the Mariners. Could be either, I thought. Or both. And I headed home from work to face more work, a taste of what's to come.

This weekend we'll bed the pipe and conduit in clean rock-free dirt, trying to avoid breakage headaches down the road. Problem is we're short on dirt, so we'll have to screen it by hand, shovelful by shovelful, enough dirt to cover four hundred feet of pipe. It'll be tedious work, exhausting, and eventually when the muscles between my shoulder blades start to wail, I will grow distracted and gaze upslope at the old wagon road: the work that came before, the work that's to come. I'm hoping it will buoy me a bit, bolster my courage, remind me of the kind of progress that is ongoing— more ditch here, a stretch of trail there—the kind of progress that might last or might not, that requires energy that is similarly tenuous: today a rock wall, tomorrow bonbons. The work will be painfully slow—the pace the polar opposite of the Jetsons'—but it will be crucial for me to imagine the finished product, the possibility of it at least, so I know if what I'm doing makes any sense. Every last damned shovelful will be an act of faith.

From the Ground On Up

❧

They arrived the summer that house building, in earnest, began. Bedecked in the latest REI fashions, wide eyed and woefully ignorant, the volunteers were, we thought at first, perfect caricatures of who we used to be. That was early on, back when Laurie and I were still fooling ourselves, imagining that we would hire a lot of the work out, that we could be kibitzers at best, phone-call makers, detail follow-uppers. At the end of the day, or a week even, we might show up at the house site and drink a cold beer and nod our approval of what had been done. That's how we pictured it. Not long after the volunteers arrived that fantasy ended. For the next two years, neither Laurie nor I would have a day off that would not be spent flailing away at some task that we knew nothing about: notching or framing or insulating wiring plumbing painting tiling. It is fair to say this: at the beginning of that summer, not one of us had the slightest idea what we were in for.

Spring was serene enough. Bare earth emerged under shallow-rooted trees, coltsfoot sprouted through the snow, and on the sunniest grassy knolls, balsam root swayed yellow and daisylike in the wind, fully realized and a good omen. At work, park managers bickered over a major bridge project stalled indefinitely by fishery concerns. They could not decide when work could be safely done. At high water, footings could not be poured. At low water, salmon would be spawning. A stalemate. Par for the course, I figured. As much evidence of the inefficacy of government as the fact that they'd hired just three of us to do all the trail work on the district—me and Phil and Jason—and tried to placate us with the meager promise of volunteers later in the summer. As if that were anything to worry over.

The unstarted house was something to worry over, not leastwise because in remote rural areas like this houses, once started, can remain unfinished indefinitely. Tar paper flaps in the wind. Lumber rots under drapes of big-leaf maple leaves. At the time I didn't understand that there could be good solid financial and artistic reasons for taking things slowly, evidence of patience and discretion, maybe even genius. Monticello, after all, remained famously unfinished during Jefferson's lifetime. I didn't know that then. I only knew that the thought of an empty weathering shell made me gnaw my fingernails to the quick. From where we stood, the project before us—building from the ground on up—looked impossibly long, an undertaking for the foolhardy or the deluded. Not a day passed that I wasn't sure we were in too deep.

Money, of course, was part of the problem. We had used our entire life savings, and we had borrowed from my family inheritance, money left by my father's stepmother, a childless woman I'd never known who lived in a trailer in South Florida and who felt beholden to her long-dead husband to pass on money to his living heirs. Such rules of conduct unnerved me and made me feel, in turn, beholden to this lonesome trailer-park woman and to the flinty immigrant ancestors before her. Do not squander this, the voices in my mind said. Finish this house if you die doing it. God help me, I meant to do it. Plans were finalized. Permits were granted. Logs were milled and decked. I held myself taut, jaws grinding, tool belt fastened.

Then the first volunteer arrived, and Jason detested her.

At twenty-four Jason was only a couple years older than the volunteers, but he'd grown up on a farm on the west side of the mountains, and he'd worked trails before. Trail work, for Jason, wasn't just a job, but an identity. He wore hickory shirts, the pin-striped cotton shirts loggers favored, and knew the names and uses of the more obscure handtools: adz, peavey, fro. He hiked as fast as anyone I'd ever known and sang Norwegian folk songs at the top of his lungs while he dragged away brush and toppled cut logs. I'd met better sawyers or riggers or brushers, but never a better, more self-consciously conscientious trail worker. He admired Darius Kinsey's black-and-white photos of the glory days of logging, the gargantuan trees, the crosscuts, the bulgy-armed grey-eyed men with wool caps and pipes. Jason looked not a little like them. He refused government housing, choosing instead to rent a screened-in gazebo, chilly and damp in the spring, where, at night, he practiced the mandolin and read Samuel Beckett, and occasionally, wrote poems.

The volunteer, Angela, moved into government housing and began complaining immediately. There were no sheets, no rugs, no saucepans, she whined. Phil's wife loaned her what she needed. Then work began. Angela was small, smaller than me even. I watched her grapple with a pick mattock on her first day, struggling to lift the heavy tool, then letting it drop, knocking away a cupful of dirt at a time. It was excruciating. We had a long five hours yet to go, and after that, for Angela, a long nine weeks. I could see that this had occurred to her, too. But what did she expect?

"I wouldn't call her mousy," Phil said to Jason and me, even though we hadn't called her that. We hadn't called her anything.

Phil defended Angela from the start. His tone sent a warning to Jason, and probably to me too, that when we're paying exactly zero, serious effort and a dearth of complaining is the most we can ask.

Jason was disgusted. But what did he expect?

Meanwhile, back at home Laurie and I had requested a bid on preparing and pouring the foundation, not leastwise because we could not face the pressure of building forms, a precise task, utterly unforgiving of errors down the road. The brothers who do that kind of work up here looked over the site and the building plans, and explained to us the high cost of hauling gravel on a barge up a lake. When one brother returned with the bid, I was home alone.

He did not even look me in the eye. He kicked a crusty patch of snow and whistled at the sky and waited while I studied the figure. I forgot he was there.

He turned to leave, then over his shoulder asked, "You want to go ahead with this then?"

I nodded. The price was exorbitant, I thought, outrageous. But what did I expect?

"Oh, and can you get power and water to the site before the pour?"

I nodded again.

The next day Laurie borrowed a neighbor's small backhoe and began to dig a four-foot-deep ditch four hundred feet from the well to the building site with the miniature bucket. She wrestled with huge rocks, balancing them atop the ridiculously tiny appendage, for an afternoon before breaking the machine and returning it for the neighbor to spot weld, a favor in return for which we'd be cutting firewood when we got a little free time. We borrowed another bigger backhoe—rented it actually, against the owner's protestations, worrying that if favors-owed kept accruing we'd be cutting firewood as very elderly ladies—and Laurie spent her weekends completing the ditch. All I could do, for a while, was stand to one side nail-biting, checking my watch. Only five months before snowfall. Move along, I thought. Move along.

As she finished I laid the water pipe and two runs of electrical conduit, gluing them together with bright purple PVC cement that inexplicably made me crave a cheeseburger every time I twisted open the lid. When at last the pipes snaked and crisscrossed into place and the backhoe disappeared into the sunset, we collapsed, victorious. This would become the story of our life, over and over like Bill Murray in *Groundhog Day*: we'd finish a job and celebrate, hugely relieved, and then awaken, always, to a new monstrous previously unconsidered task, this time bedding the pipes. We placed five-gallon buckets under homemade screens—chicken wire and two by fours. And we shoveled. If we could. Along most of the ditch the rocks were too big to move, so we scraped dirt off with the shovels, a desperate futile sound. As we filled the buckets we dumped the rockless dirt over the water pipe and conduit in the ditch, trying to prevent friction holes from wearing into the hammering pipes over time. We stuck to this scrape-and-shovel routine after work and on the weekends until eventually electricity was hooked up, and water ran through the spigot, and Laurie wept with relief, and a date was set for the brothers to pour the foundation. Only problem was they'd be short handed.

We took the day off to spend the day dumping ninety-pound bags of cement by hand—Laurie on one side, me on the other—into a portable cement mixer while one brother added gravel with a miniloader. The process is dictated by remoteness and by the uneven terrain, and it is one the brothers have perfected—noisy and sloppy and precarious, graceful as a dance—over many years. The mixer mixes and then fills a hopper. Another brother lifts the hopper with his boom truck and delivers it to his eighteen-year-old son balancing on the forms, and the son grabs the hopper and yanks open a stubborn release lever so that a half-yard can splooge between his boots and into place. It did not take long to realize it was worth every penny. At lunch, the job nearly complete, the crew sat on rocks and upturned buckets amidst the barmy sloughs and puddles of cement mud. Laurie served coffee. I had to leave. It was my turn to go to the boat landing to pick up another volunteer.

❧

Three kinds of volunteers work on trails. First are the day trippers, professionals mostly, joiners, members of the Sierra Club or the Boeing Alpine Club or the Backcountry Horsemen, who arrive in armies to work for a day. They accomplish a bit, get sore, and go home. I used to lead groups like this when I worked for the Forest Service. They were nice folks generally, though there were exceptions, like the Boeing engineer who insisted on pounding straight down, over and over, with an axe onto a small log across the trail, beating on the thing, pummeling it. I tried to interrupt long enough to show him how much more effective an axe is when you chop at an angle.

"Get out of my way, little girl," he said.

I left him alone.

"It can't be chopped," he announced half an hour later.

He tossed the axe into the mud, where I recovered it and chopped the log out in a few swift strokes, more show-offy than I would normally be, but in that situation, vindicated.

Then there are the troubled youth—Hoods in the Woods—for whom trail work can be a kind of punishment. The powers that be decide that troubled youth sitting all day at juvie playing hoops and watching the tube does no damned good. Swinging a pick axe? Now you're talking. Besides, says the kinder gentler perspective, the woods are healing. Once the volunteers breathe fresh air and take in the majestic views, they will be rehabilitated, cured in fact. Moreover, the liberals argue, this work is career preparation. Never mind that the jobs it prepares a person for, without a college education, are few and far between, seasonal and low paying, and usually hogged by college-educated nature freaks like us, underemployed by choice.

Once I camped in an alpine meadow with a group of hoods who huddled in their tents after work with cans of Raid they'd packed up the mountain in hopes of keeping their camp bug-free. When we tried to coax them out to watch the dramatic sunset, they refused.

"Nobody told me nothin' about no mountains. Nobody told me nothin' about no bugs," one guy explained.

They were there, we discovered, because they'd been promised that they could go to flagger school when they were finished, after which they could work for the state highway department for a wage three times what those of us who were paid to do trail work were getting. Those hoods were not fools. They shook their heads and zipped their tents.

The third kind of volunteers, the kind we had that summer—the kind I was once upon a time—are fresh out of college and at loose ends. For them, volunteering on trails, like joining the Peace Corps, offers escape and service and adventure. The park baldly exploits these college kids by making them do the work of paid employees for nothing ("scabs," one longtime seasonal calls them). For the volunteers, it's a fair enough trade since in return they get free housing and transportation and a weekly stipend. They get, in short, a summer in paradise. For the government, it's not quite as good a deal. By the time the volunteers are trained and coddled and cajoled into physical condition, usually, they have to leave. Their net worth often comes out in the red. But they look good on paper, and if they want to come, who's to turn them away? I didn't invite the volunteers, but at least half the time, I'd be in charge of them. So I rinsed my forearms under the miracle spigot, and sped off to the boat landing.

Drew stepped off the boat, a new backpack slung over one shoulder, and offered his hand in greeting. He was friendly and polite and clearly distracted by the scenery: the lake shimmering green in the sun, the snow lingering on the north-facing slopes, the endless fringe of treetops, so tall, fingering up the mountainsides. I apologized for my cement-dust clothes and I asked about his life. He'd come straight from D.C. where he'd been working as an editor, a job I sometimes think I'd like to have.

"Wow," he said. "It's great to be away from there."

I drove him up the road to the ramshackle trailer that would be his home for the summer. I pulled open the stubborn sliding-glass door to a musty room filled with surplused military furniture and a wheezing off-balance refrigerator.

"This is awesome," he said. He meant it. "See you tomorrow."

Quin and Lisa, the last of the four, arrived a week or so later. Quin was taciturn, Midwestern, named after a college basketball player not too many years older than me. He only spoke when he stooped to admire wildflowers.

"What is this?" he'd ask.

"Lupine."

Twenty minutes of silence.

"What is this?"

He fingered the delicate petals.

"Some kind of penstemon," I said. "I don't know which."

Lisa smiled too much. She was very nice, the epitome of nice. So nice she made Jason squirm. This was not the stuff of Darius Kinsey. Not the stuff of Samuel Beckett. Or so he thought. Lisa took on tasks enthusiastically, competently, and was surprisingly strong, and generally, surprising. Turned out she had, before volunteering on trails, been working in forensics. She described autopsies in vivid detail in the same sweet voice that greets the birds in a Disney cartoon.

"Gall stones," she told us once, "shine like multi-colored pearls." And, she added, if you do them after the breasts, the bile cleans up all the fat on the table. "Like that," she said and snapped her fingers.

🦎

On Fridays, my day off, I drove six miles to the public satellite phone and dialed a mobile phone in Prineville, Oregon. Who knows what Lance thought of us? We'd driven to visit his operation two winters before on Phil's recommendation. Lance met us, sun-squinting in a derby and a clean white shirt, jeans and logging boots. He was a local boy who had started this log home company, an ingenious use for the plentiful local juniper, and he oversaw the whole operation himself: marketing, design, milling, transport, and sometimes, construction. That February morning, he drove us around for four hours, over a skiff of new snow, though we hardly looked like big-money customers, to show us the tiny log cabins— Line Shacks, he called them—that he had built at the local state parks.

We liked the cabins a lot. We liked everything about them. We liked the small operation, and we secretly liked the word "kit," the paddy-cake simplicity it connoted. We liked the idea of using trees that were being removed for ecological reasons, because they guzzled up native wetlands, trees that would otherwise be chained away—dragged between two bulldozers—to be used for firewood or sometimes just burned in place. Bucking the stuff up could dull a saw chain down to nubbins. And we were lured by the uniqueness of the wood itself, hard and knotty and swirled yellow-orange. But there's no doubt about it: we were also lured by Lance.

He took us to lunch at a local tavern where, when we ordered ribs and Buds, he was visibly relieved.

"I didn't know," he admitted, "if you'd be vegetarians."

We grinned and gnawed on the meat, glad to buck the burden of stereotype, and I studied Lance for any trace of malice. There was none. Whatever he thought about us, he remained honest and good natured, matter of fact.

"You can put one of these places up in a day," he said, a salesman at heart and a believer.

I didn't believe him for a second.

From that point on, the Friday calls became ritual. I kept a list of questions scribbled on a steno pad. How do you affix hurricane braces? What size lag screw? What type of plywood? What gauge wire? Every week there'd be a half dozen new questions, most that had nothing to do with the log part of the house whatsoever, and Lance would answer them succinctly in his friendly drawl, communicating across twenty-four thousand miles of outer space from mobile phone to satellite phone and back again. It was a tenuous unlikely connection. But it worked.

When it got closer to time to put up the walls, the promised one-day log raising, I called Lance and begged him to come help us.

"You can do it yourself," he said again.

"We want you to come," I said.

"OK," he said. "OK."

So we ordered a keg and sent out postcards inviting twenty or so people from the valley with varying levels of expertise to a work party. We invited men and women, coworkers and neighbors. We invited Phil and Jason, but conspicuously, did not invite any of the volunteers

❧

Not that it bothered them much. The volunteers had enough to worry about adjusting to trail work. They swamped a little, dug a few drains, took their brush whips in hand gamely, if not exactly enthusiastically. Then it was time to camp.

On our first trip out, Angela lagged behind.

"Women," she told me, "have less endurance than men. Don't you think?" We were a half mile in on a six-mile backpack into camp, and she had sat on a stump to catch her breath.

"No," I argued, this being a rather sore subject with me, "Actually women have greater endurance than men. Think about childbirth." I pressed my point more than I like to, I admit.

Angela sometimes brought out the worst in me. "Men might be stronger, but women have more endurance. Come on." I had not sat down, and I don't like to stand still with a heavy pack on. It's very hard on my upper back.

"Doesn't this hurt your shoulders?" As if she'd read my mind.

"It does hurt my shoulders," I tried to explain, "but not enough to complain about." I sighed. "Sometimes, if you are less strong or less skilled, the only thing you can do to prove yourself is to not complain."

I felt like I had betrayed a deep part of myself, given voice to a code that should never be spoken aloud. I worried about this. I shouldn't have, because Angela hadn't listened.

"Well," Angela said. "It hurts my shoulders."

I turned on my heels and marched toward the next switchback.

That night we gathered around the campfire. We talked about backpacking food—which soup packets we favored, which noodles, how to get enough protein as a vegetarian, which they were all, predictably, in varying stages of becoming. And we talked about books. Jason squirmed at the predictability of their reading list—*Zen and the Art of Motorcycle Maintenance, Encounters with the Archdruid, Siddhartha, The Monkey Wrench Gang*. They'd fallen into a perfect niche, the ideology of the nature quest, wherein by venturing into the wilderness you find, well, something— adventure, redemption, enlightenment. Now here they were, around a campfire in a lodgepole thicket at four thousand feet, wondering what comes next. Their fears trickled out between bites of ramen.

The guys dreaded the paths that seemed most open to them: that Quin would follow in his father's footsteps and be a stockbroker, that Drew would lug his English degree back to graduate school and an academic career. Lisa aspired, actually, to be a doctor, but feared she wasn't smart or committed enough. Angela had another semester of school on the East Coast, a boyfriend, and she was afraid she couldn't face staying there when she finished, though she didn't know exactly where she'd go instead. Compared with the alternatives, trail work was looking better and better.

"You guys've got it made," Drew said, looking at Jason and me. "This is the good life."

Jason folded his arms across his chest and tried not to scowl.

I considered taking his cue, changing my tack and telling the volunteers, in no uncertain terms, that this life is not as easy as it seems. An eight-month trail season is a whole lot longer than a three-month season, I could say. There are strings of weeks when your boots never dry. There are bloody smashed fingers and bulging off-kilter vertebrae and the awkward early-morning hobble to the coffee pot when plantar fasciitis inevitably sets in. It is not summer camp! I wanted to say. I looked around the campfire at the volunteers nursing their blistered toes and stretching their backs, and I knew that they saw that for themselves. They just weren't complaining. They respected me, I think, and wanted to impress me, and that summer more than any I'd worked before, that meant a lot.

"I gotta figure out what I'm gonna do," Angela said, more or less speaking for all of them.

"You've got time," I said. "I haven't come close to figuring out where I'm going."

"You're building a house," Angela said. "You're not going anywhere."

I laughed. "You've got a point."

ᕦᕦ

True enough. We were building our own home, my girlfriend and I, and the baggage slung onto that phrase—"building our own home" more than "venturing into the wilderness" or even than "my girlfriend and I"—was, we found, massive and multifaceted.

You can't tell people you're building a house without a preconceived idea fixing in their minds. There's the bright light of recognition—a dream house!—gleaned from *Sunset*, *Martha Stewart*, and *Log Home Living*: snuggly great rooms with recessed lighting and hand-stitched quilts and labs on their own monogrammed cedar beds. People familiar with the genre ask questions like: What lighting fixtures will you choose? What kind of cabinets? There are so many decisions, the dream housers say, and they are thinking about doorknobs and window trim, carpet colors, and tile. These decisions were, for us, so distant that they seem unreal, superfluous, hardly pertinent. We were still mired in concerns about structural integrity and proper ventilation, about soffit screens and new drill bits and caulking.

And those concerns invited another label: do-it-yourselfers. People like this idea. It's so self-reliant, individualistic. It's so spunky. When I lay down at night, I would obsess, replaying the details of what the next steps should be: walls, joists, rafters, sheath. This four million times a night: walls, joists, rafters, sheath. Then folks would pore over our plans and ask: Why such a beefy ridge beam? Why such a narrow staircase? These were tinkerers, full-time DIYs, the kind of people for whom how things should go together is a state of mind, not one that they have to repeat to themselves, mantra like, when they ought to be sleeping. They would ask. And I would reply: I don't know. Over and over and over.

Here was the worst of it—the sore subject again—people were impressed, I knew, not just because we knew so little or because we tried so hard, but because we're, well, girls. We'd send friends photos of ourselves at work on the house, and I'd feel a little silly, as if we had been posing at those cut-outs that allow you to put your face in the body of a cowboy or a hippopotamus. It felt like play-acting, and it didn't help a bit when I began to realize that we'd been at it so long, and so continually, that the play-acting—dream housers, DIYs—was running the distinct danger of becoming reality.

ᶜᵂ

Preparations for the work party were many. We hired out the subfloor to the same neighbor who had milled our trees into logs. He and his son—a lanky teenager who made the heavy work look downright easy—finished the job swiftly and professionally.

"You could drive a truck on this," the son called to us, stomping down hard on the new platform.

We rented a hammer drill to set bolts to affix the logs to the foundation and negotiated with Lance for a log truck on a run to Spokane to drop our logs downlake. Eventually, the logs showed up on the barge.

And Lance showed up, too. He drove seven hours and hopped a float plane to get here. He demonstrated how to stack logs between the ten-inch posts, tape on strips of insulation—the shape and diameter of french fries, but longer—then drive log screws into place, brace the wall and start the next one. Paddy-cake stuff.

There were more hands than necessary, so there was plenty of kibitzing and coffee drinking, and there was a cacophony of chainsaws running, hammers pounding, kids and dogs howling underfoot. One friend brought a camcorder and caught the day on film—the laughter and the frenzy and the tall firs swaying in the wind, and my labored head-shaking grin. You can see it even as I stack and drill logs, and pull extension cords round, and lift the major cross beams. You can see that I still do not believe the house will be built. Even at the end of the day, the end of the tape, when I look so relieved, ecstatic, posing for a group photo with so many friends and dogs and kids—such mayhem!—even then you can see I do not believe. Later, my mom will show that video to half of southern California, to anyone she can get to watch, so proud will she be. And, my deep eyebrow furrows aside, this is how it looks on tape: as if the whole house went up in a single day, at a party, between pizza lunch and salmon supper. Just like that.

The next morning Lance will have an hour to spare, and we will beg him to set one last particularly tricky angled beam into place. He'll wipe cinnamon roll crumbs from his beard, sit atop one post and lock his elbow to hold the chainsaw steady, then saw a flawless notch into the juniper post five feet across from him. Then I'll drive him to the dock, where he'll tip his derby and step back onto the float plane, leaving me awestruck and unspeakably grateful.

❧

Trail season wore on into August with the temperature holding fast in triple digits, the black flies swarming, the brush encroaching. The volunteers settled into routine. I saw them on their weekends lounging at the local bakery with ice cream cones or riding bikes with fishing poles or going day hiking—hiking of all things!—into the high country, undaunted by the heat or bugs. They'd holler and wave to us working away at the house site, give us the ol' thumbs up. I was buoyed by their good humor. Maybe their goofy enthusiasm was contagious. Or maybe their romantic view of my life made my life seem more romantic to me, the way Darius Kinsey photos made Jason feel more romantic about trail work. Everything, to them, was a story in the making.

On one trip Quin and Drew decided to make their packs lighter by supplementing their food with native berries. The huckleberry bushes were putting out a bumper crop that summer. Berries were everywhere, plump and sweet, large as grapes and weighing down the plants. Though Quin and Drew's lips turned purple with the effort, the berry experiment was a failure. They could not possibly eat enough of them. Around the campfire, Jason silently distributed slabs from his summer sausage.

On another trip, we built a new log crib for a cable bridge, a Lincoln Log set-up twelve feet by twelve feet by four feet high, that, once built, needed to be filled with rocks. I sent the volunteers to collect rocks, and each of them returned with one rock, tossed it in the crib, and stood awaiting directions. "More rocks," I said. Again they returned with one rock apiece. After that, I handed Jason the chainsaw to finish the notching, while I joined the rock collectors.

"See," I said, throwing in an armload, "this whole thing has to be filled with rocks."

Drew looked at me incredulously. "All the way?" he asked.

Not, of course, that the volunteers were the only ones capable of foolishness. One night Jason passed around The Power, a homemade liquor he'd brought back from a winter trip to Africa along with a catalog of obscure ailments and a not-so-obscure lousy gut. The Power went to my head and I stayed up late by the fire and did not notice the temperature dropping precipitously. I completely forgot that Laurie had convinced me to carry a sheet instead of a sleeping bag to lighten my load until I found myself lying flat on my back in my tent, in all my clothes, teeth chattering, laughing at myself.

The next day I decided to have Angela and Lisa to help me move a large root wad—a dirt-encrusted whorl that tore out of the earth when a two-hundred-foot-tall fir blew over. We'd cut the tree earlier in the season. Now the root wad sat in the middle of the trail. Lisa and Angela and I chopped into the tread to break what few roots still held, then grubbed around a bit with pulaskis among the interwoven zags of upturned roots to remove the dirt and rocks, the excess weight. Then we pushed on it a bit, checking the leverage, deciding which direction it might roll. It was exactly the kind of brute-strength job that normally Phil would avoid dumping on us. But Phil was not with us, so I was the boss, and it felt liberating to be working away from the house on something I actually knew how to do, something that might look overwhelming to the volunteers, but that might actually prove to be, in do-gooder terms, empowering. Brute strength, I wanted to show them, is overrated. Size is not everything. Neither is gender, nor age. Not even pay status. Finally we lay on our backs and pushed with our legs, and cheered when the root wad toppled, end over end, off the trail down the side hill toward the creek below.

Drew and Quin tried not to act surprised when we caught up to them an hour later, ready for the rest of the day of work. Jason ignored us. For one thing, he knew we could handle the job. It was not all that hard. For another, he didn't think Angela needed much empowerment. The main reason he ignored us, though, was Lisa. She was just too nice, he'd say. And, I'd noticed, she'd begun to show symptoms of a crush on Jason, even as Quin had a miserable, too-obvious crush on her. Late in the summer when a fire call came, Lisa and Quin both packed their bags. (This the consolation prize for volunteering: that you might be trained as a firefighter to work as an emergency hire for a two-week hitch on the fireline.) At the last minute, fire managers decided that they only needed one firefighter, not two. Only Lisa went. Quin sulked visibly for two weeks, because, he said, he had wanted to fight a fire so badly, and sure, we'd go for that. His crush was too transparent and debilitating to ridicule. So we worked short handed, one volunteer lost to firefighting and another sick with longing, one disgruntled paid employee, and another—me—utterly preoccupied.

❧

Only walls were up and September hovered just around the bend. Money was running low. When it turned out that by plain dumb luck a carpenter neighbor who'd work cheap was available, I was euphoric. That he would take us on as his unskilled laborers was both icing on the cake and utterly terrifying.

Bob is an athlete, an expert skier and mountaineer and sailor who started doing carpentry, I'd imagine, because it gave him the freedom to take days off, but after two decades he'd become a skilled cabinet maker and a boat builder who showed his work in local art shows. Bob had also been an army ranger in his youth and maintained a hard unsympathetic edge in his distinctly hippie existence. Each summer he'd take a group of youngish kids on challenging cross-country mountaineering trips on which he was, by all parental accounts, utterly merciless. When you ask any of the kids—the Bob Scouts, people call them—they'll tell you the trip was the time of their lives. We did have some idea of what we were getting into.

Laurie worked first. She and Bob began setting second-floor joists. The hard locally milled lumber that would make up all the non-kit house members—joists, rafters, interior walls—required pre-drilling before being screwed into place, so the job required working on ladders double holstered, a cordless drill on each hip.

"Never drop a cordless drill. If you drop it, it's finished," he said.

Laurie dropped them several times, panicking each time. Bob just kept working. No damage done.

Over time, we got better with the drills, and with everything else. We learned how to measure correctly, to saw precisely, and to move quickly, very quickly always. We handled hammers and clamps and levels and squares, gaining confidence as we went along, until there we were beating stout twenty-penny nails like bridge spikes into the hard local fir. There was satisfaction in the numbers, all those fractions of fractions, and in the clean angles, advantages you rarely have on trails where you work with native materials, logs usually, and a chainsaw. (In the shack we'd built our own furniture and a small addition, but we'd joked that we did it all with a chainsaw, the only tool we knew how to use. It was not far from the truth.) And there was frustration, too.

Bob would hand me a task, then turn away. If it got too quiet, if the hammering stilled, he'd know without looking that I'd made a mistake, and holler over his shoulder without turning his head:

"Get the crowbar, Ana Maria."

It was humiliating and invigorating, and we were, at the end of each day, equal parts exhausted and exultant. The sky deepened into rich September blue, the temperature dropped to the eighties, and there before our eyes, a skeleton was rising from the ground. A house. A house. I used vacation days or traded days, missing a day of trails during the week to lift rafters into place, then on the weekend packing a couple chainsaws and some spikes to camp ahead of the crew, or racing out with Jason on a make-up day to build a quick footbridge. Anything to get the roof on. Roof on. Roof on. It became the mantra.

Bob liked working with us, you could tell. We were comic relief in part, determined like little children, pursing our lips, sticking our tongues out in concentration, smashing fingers, hurrying to keep up. We stayed late each night after he left to sweep away the mounds of sawdust and organize the tools. And we played new music, a lot that he'd never heard of since he's ten years older than we are and had been sequestered in the woods for a lot longer. After work, sometimes, his wife would join us and their two-year-old would run around with tools and pound on the staircase or the newly constructed walls, and we would sit and talk about the next step in the game, and wallow in the rich smells of fresh-cut fir and juniper. Back in the shack we slept the sleep of the dead.

Visitors came in hoards; neighbors with whom we had been on nodding terms before now came bearing generous gifts of compliments or loaned tools. They whistled through their teeth. Nice spot you got here. And our families came too. When you don't have kids, we found, house-building is a sure sign of adulthood achieved. Settled, they'd whisper. Those girls are getting settled. Relatives we'd not seen since childhood materialized: Laurie's great-aunt from Chicago, in her seventies, a woman who famously detests the outdoors; my cousins and aunt and uncle from St. Louis who'd never seen such a place. We stopped work often to give tours of the skeleton. With the relatives, we took days off to raft the river or to take a motorboat ride, to barbecue and try to pretend that we were not wracked by the pressure, always, every minute.

Unsolicited help appeared, too, out of nowhere and out of everywhere. A neighbor built a temporary power pole from a discarded "Dock Closed" sign and taught us to wire it. Laurie's brother used precious vacation days to help, and a footloose cousin of theirs backpacked into the valley and spent two days collecting facing rocks from amid the rubble. Friends on their way to take a hike helped haul floor joists—two by tens—from the stickered pile into the house, a job that took several hours while a storm brewed. Too late for the trailhead, they huddled with us under the new porch, watching the rain spatter off newly exposed rocks. When it was time for the rafters, Laurie's boss helped lug the two by twelves to the second floor in stifling heat. A crew materialized each time we had to lift something particularly heavy, four or six or eight people heaving beams into place, staying long enough to pose for a snapshot, then wishing us luck and moving on.

A friend of mine from college, a contractor by profession, showed up with a cartful of discarded tools from his industrial jobsite. And he brought, by far, the best building advice we ever got. I told him about a concern I had, some blocking I think it was, along the rim joists between the pine beam and the second-floor deck on which the gable end would be constructed. Should I do it? He shrugged.

I mean, I explained, I think I should have done it, but I had not. I did not tell him the truth that I had stayed up half the night worrying about this. He shrugged again.

"Don't kid yourself," he said. "Building a house is all one big mistake."

He knew. He and his wife had taken a handful of years to build their own home on Vashon Island in the Puget Sound. Now they were back to life as usual. They arrived late on a Friday and camped with their two-year-old while it dumped rain, then crowded into the shack for meals, taking it all in stride. On Saturday the rain let up, and my college friend tossed plywood sheets down onto joists, gobs of Liquid Nails dripping along the seams, then Bob leaped with a snowboarder's pizzazz to get the tongue in the groove, and Laurie and I drilled mightily, screwing the floor down as fast as we could to keep up. By suppertime the floor was on. Another celebration.

It was run-of-the-mill stuff, I know, hardly worth the bravado, but it was the first time we'd done such a thing, and the first time we would have a house, a home, stayputtedness, and our friends were part of it, of course, as were the heat and bugs and rain. If we had hired it out entirely, as we had hoped, or if we had somehow— god knows how—over decades, done it entirely ourselves, it would not have been the same.

"It was," my mom liked to brag to her friends at one of those mandatory showings of the wall-raising video, "a real community effort."

I cringed when she'd say it because I always cringe at statements like that—over-simplified and full of idealism—and because, after all, it was largely our transparent helplessness and our own shameless begging for help, our own planning and our own bumbling efforts that dragged the house up from the ground. But I never contradicted her because I knew, despite everything, she was right.

Bob's already fast pace got even faster whenever help arrived, making the most of the bodies at hand. When, one day, Phil showed up just as Bob and I finished setting rafters, Bob waved him onto the roof. Time to sheath. Bob climbed the ladder with a sheet of plywood balanced on one hip and passed it to us, and Phil and I balanced across the new steep roof (a 10/12 pitch to let the snow slide), not looking down, never looking down, set the plywood and nailed it in place. By the time we were done with one, Bob was back with another, and by the end of that day, all but the dormer was sheathed. For that, Laurie would take over with help from her brother, who'd take more time off work. Before long, it was October, and the house was sheathed, and sheets of metal roofing sat bundled on the driveway. Nothing could stop us.

Progress was in the wind. The bureaucrats had even negotiated a compromise to allow the bridge contractors to divert the river during high water to pour footings. Now, as spawning season approached, the stringers were already in place, so all the work could take place above the water, out of the way of the salmon. The expensive bridge contract was moving ahead whole hog. I was impressed and emboldened by the sight of it, the heavy steel beams mimicking the ancient timbers of the previous historic bridge perfectly, just as I hoped our prefabbish kit house might give the impression of woodsiness.

One night on the way home from trail work with Lisa, who by then was back from two weeks of firefighting in Montana, I saw Bob's pickup stopped at the bridge site. Bob looked a bit sheepish, and the contractor he was talking to looked downright sinister. The contractor leered at me, I swear it, though I'd never met the man, as Bob walked toward the trails rig and motioned for me to roll down the window.

They were hiring locals, Bob explained. He'd been waiting to hear. This, it finally occurred to me, explained how someone with his skills had still been looking for work in early September.

I let out a stream of curses and tried to hold back tears.

"You'll get the roof on," Bob scoffed. "You can do it on your own."

I stared at the steering wheel.

"I'll help you on my days off," he said. I knew better. His days off would be precisely the days he'd want to work for the contractor: the overtime days, the Sunday differential. The bridge guys were paying forty dollars an hour straight time, I knew. We'd been paying fifteen under the table.

Lisa smiled weakly.

You know the situation is grim when even the epitome of niceness can't think of one thing to say.

🐇

There was nothing to do, then, but trail work. Angela's season ended early as it had begun. She'd done fine, Phil insisted, just fine. Then Drew and Quin took paying jobs on a trail-construction project on the west side. Lisa opted to stay. Phil had left on vacation, so for a while it would be just me and Lisa and Jason. Jason was not thrilled. The season had worn him thin, the distance from his westside home had stretched with news of a grandmother's death, and the gazebo was growing colder in the pre-dawn dark. The last dregs of romance were leeching out of him like so much booze shared by the campfire.

On top of that we had been assigned a somewhat dubious task: moving rocks to divert a creek that sometimes ran down a short section of trail. We had rock bars and picks. Mostly we tossed round river rocks from one channel to another. There was way too much time to think. So we talked. We talked about music, and they lectured me some because of my age and my ignorance. For hours the discussion centered on butt rock, a subgenre apparently, which I'd never heard of.

"So is AC/DC butt rock? I saw them in concert, you know."

"Yeah, with Blue Oyster Cult. You told us already. Yeah, sort of, but it's more like Motley Crue and Ratt," Jason said.

"What about Nirvana?"

"The antithesis," said Lisa.

"Green Day, then?"

"Yes," said Jason .

"No way," said Lisa.

There was, sometimes, tension between them I couldn't read.

One day, the government bridge job hit a temporary roadblock. Bob showed up, true to his word, at the trails shop in the morning, suddenly available to teach us how to put the metal roofing on. So I took the day off, leaving Jason and Lisa to their own devices. Later I'd learn it did not go well.

‹

Bob showed Laurie and me the procedure, nothing too tricky: haul a twenty-foot-long, foot-wide metal sheet up the ladder, set it in place, then kick the lip of one sheet over the seam of the last one. Screw the sheet in place with the cordless drill that you have not yet dropped today, that you have not dropped, actually, in weeks. Voila! What amazed us was not that Bob thought this was easy, but that we did too. In a few short months, we had been transformed. The only remaining problem was that it was hard for Laurie and me to take days off at the same time. We were walking a thin line, using the most vacation time we possibly could without threatening what little job security we had. So one Friday, after Bob had gone back to the bridge and Laurie had gone to work, Jason climbed onto the roof to help me with the last sections of metal—the very last! It was a gorgeous fall day. Yellow cottonwood leaves fluttered in the wind. Wood smoke mingled with the scent of decomposing spawned-out fish.

While we worked Jason told me the story of his talk with Lisa.

"What do you have against me?" Lisa had asked. It had been coming down to that, I suppose, for weeks.

"It's not you, exactly. It's volunteers."

Jason had to explain himself. And he tried it this way: Lisa wanted to be a doctor, right? Well, what would she think if somebody just showed up in surgery, say, or in the emergency room to "volunteer"? She would not stand for it, would she? They were not trained; they were not professionals; all they would do is keep the doctors from doing what they had to do.

I understood Jason's point. I'd considered it myself, back with that axe-happy Boeing guy: how obnoxious it was to presume that our job required no skill. I used to imagine driving down to Boeing, announcing I was there to volunteer, daring this stranger to be anything but grateful, and plopping down to smack away at his computer keyboard. But I'd always known, in my heart of hearts, that trail work is pretty menial stuff.

"I'm really sorry," I said. I wasn't sure if I was sorry for Jason or for Lisa or for the whole ugly situation.

Jason and I finished the roofing in short order, a kind of anticlimax, and we sat on the porch looking across at the knobby ridges. A few hundred feet high, they are only the first gentle steps on the way into these craggy mountains. I thought about how much like life those ridges were: how they level out to fool you, how, when you're on top of one, you never see the section around the bend, steeper yet and punctuated by cliffs, and beyond that glaciers, crevasses, so many dangers. It had been easier to believe the volunteers were less than me before I started building the house and life went topsy-turvy. Because of that—because for so many months I hadn't been sure, exactly, where I stood or what I was capable of or where I'd end up, because I had been utterly at the mercy of people who knew more than I —I had more in common, right then, with the volunteers than I'd ever have wanted to admit.

Not that I hadn't expected any of this. I had wanted to hurry the house, I realized now, not just because of money or precedent but in large part because I wanted to rush the upheaval. Get it over with. I had started house building with my eyes scrunched tight, waiting for it end—like a roller coaster ride, or a trip to the dentist— the way perhaps Angela had seen the trail season. But it never comes off that tidily. There would be, eventually, details I'd wish we had concentrated on. There'd be too much drywall, not enough tile, irregular soffits, a too-small mud room. Minor things really, hardly worth the mention, except to say that, as the year went by, I'd find myself changed—more humble, more patient.

"Look at this," Jason said at last, breaking the silence with his most exuberantly loud voice and sweeping his arm toward the horizon. "You've got it made."

I looked at him, checking to see if he was being facetious, if this were another jab at the starry-eyed volunteers, or maybe at me, at how stodgy he could foresee me becoming. His face betrayed nothing of the sort. He looked generous and hopeful and utterly believing.

"We do," I said. "We really do."

◅

November descended with the familiar icy grey inversion that would last, but for snowstorms, until March. Laurie and I drove to the landing, stopping to recruit friends along the way, and it was a good thing because it took six of us to lift the pallet with the new woodstove into the back of the pickup, then six of us again to lift it off the pickup and haul it into the house to where Laurie had built a small rock hearth. We set the stove in place, where it awaited a full day of stovepipe fitting and fussing, then we drove our friends home, knowing it would not be the last time we'd have to ask them for help. There would be so much more to do, so much more to learn, as we took on more of the tasks ourselves: insulating, wiring, plumbing, hanging and mudding drywall, staining the trim, chinking the logs. In winter we'd huddle by this stove daily, burning lumber scraps, sipping mugs of tea during short breaks from the work, wondering when, if ever, the house would be warm enough.

◅

Another year. That's all. We moved in on summer solstice and chipped away at the details on our weekends. By the following winter, I could sit inside in a T-shirt, deliciously idle, surrounded by the rich yellow warmth of wood, and the warmth of the fire— the warmth of a bathtub, if I so chose, such novelty!—a cat in my lap and a pallet for a kitchen table. The good life.

Jason, meanwhile, bought his grandmother's farmhouse out on the flat fertile floodplains feeding Puget Sound. On his weekends he makes repairs on it. What we went through in one clean swipe, he tells us, he is wed to for life. When he needs a break, a couple times a year, he comes to visit.

Lisa never did go to medical school. That winter she moved in with a firefighter she had met on her stint in Montana in the upper reaches of the Bitterroot Valley. Maybe what had threatened Jason most, what I missed entirely, was that she was becoming one of us. It was, for her—who would've known?—the summer that changed her life.

Where Drew and Quin ended up, I've never heard.

Only Angela returned for a second season, not on trail crew but at the local bakery where, the bakery owner attested, she turned out to be a helluva worker, showing up for the 4 a.m. shift day after day. I didn't see her much. I don't make it to the bakery that often. When Laurie and I ran into her at a music festival in Seattle, a mad crush of bodies on Labor Day weekend, Angela visited with us for a while then asked which bands we were going to see. She giggled when we mentioned Modest Mouse, a newer alternativish band.

"What?" Laurie asked. "What?"

I knew what Angela meant. You're too old for that, she thought. And she was too weak for trails, we used to think. And house building was impossible. Maybe it's all a matter of proving the assumptions wrong. It'd be easy to miss—how far we've come—if there weren't some reference point, if Angela weren't standing right there, so defiant, so undeniably strong, explaining her plans to stay out West and get herself a job at the food co-op in Bellingham, her ties to the past broken, like ours have been, by happenstance and a short spurt of misery. We've got it made, I thought. All of us. As if it were predestined—Meant To Be in some New Agey Calvinist conflation—and not the result of miles walked, nails pounded, phone calls made, help and advice and sympathy offered.

Don't kid yourself, I remind myself. It's all one big mistake

Winter Driving

⚜

Indulge me here. Let me let me glamorize it one more time—*what a long strange trip it's been*—because my winters spent driving in circles are nearly past. (My inner-adult interrupts: Phew! I'm glad that's over!) And because, maybe, I'm not ready to see them go. It was a backwards sort of freedom, I know, the freedom to leave the beautiful places where I spent the summer—wilderness areas and national parks—to drive through wind and snow and rain and lousy visibility to no place in particular, but it was freedom nonetheless, freedom from having to work, to be at loose ends, homeless (or mostly so), braving the ice-sheened interstate, or more often, the snow-packed state road winding beside a frozen creek, the sky unchanging gray, the radio alternating from Jesus to Paul Harvey. Sometimes I pretended it was the destination that mattered, but that was not true. I was always depressed by the glitz of ski towns, wearied by the monotony of family visits, embarrassed by pay-phone calls to long-lost friends in Jackson Hole or Winter Park: Remember me? Can I stay at your place next Tuesday? It was the road itself that was exhilarating and exhausting, that was, for me, a sort of wilderness.

My family planted the seed. When I was a kid, we took the requisite cross-country trips: five of us in a station wagon from L.A. to St. Louis with stops aplenty: the Grand Canyon and the Gateway Arch, the Corn Palace and Wall Drug. We visited Circus Circus in Las Vegas for an hour while our crayons melted on the dashboard. We stayed at Little America, the massive tourist village in Wyoming that sported a golf course and an amusement park and gift shops crammed with newspapers announcing: The King

is Dead! What king? Elvis had died. Who was Elvis? I carried a
tape player, an old pre-Walkman type, with me at all times, and I
hunkered in the way-back listening to the Monkees as I watched
the scenery streaming by. The way-back is where I learned the
twofold spell of the horizon: full of promise and, like the end of
the rainbow, utterly unreachable. It was intoxicating as a Davy Jones
tambourine solo, and I was addicted.

There was history on the road—the wagon ruts along the Oregon
trail reaching out for the elusive horizon, still, after all those years.
And there was, of course, the present. At Mt. Rushmore my sister
and I dashed through the parking lot playing the license plates
game. Well into the trip we had seen maybe ten of the fifty states,
but at Mt. Rushmore we saw them all! Even Alaska and Hawaii!
We were dumbfounded, elated; we didn't give a hoot about the
presidential rocks. In fact, we were rather lukewarm on the subject
of rocks in general. We had seen so many Southwest parks that
one year we refused to get out of the car, chanting "No more rock
formations. No more rock formations." What I did care about were
books and the worlds they opened. One year I wanted to visit
Walnut Grove, Laura Ingall's real little house on the prairie, and in
a rolly-hilled cranny of Minnesota, miles from anywhere, there it
was! There it was!

And, though none of us knew it at the time, there on the blacktop
between the white line and the yellow lay large chunks of my future.
When we arrived home, I traced our routes onto an auto club map
sloppily with fat magic markers, then taped the map to my bedroom
wall. Routes we took more than once I retraced to made them look
fatter, to show that we were old hands out there, veterans of a
kind—on I-70 through Colorado, say, or I-40 through Kansas. If I
had stuck with that practice over the years certain roads, like I-5
from Canada to Mexico, would be wide as my forearm.

⚫

Thinking about road trips, I get to thinking that maybe we, the naturey ones among us, give specific places, particularly real pretty places, way too much credit. These places—wilderness areas, national parks—are supposed to transform us, make us new. I speak from some experience, and with no small measure of shame, when I say that they do not continuously dispense spiritual wowness like a fountain. When I first started spending summers in the woods, I was full of ideas: you oughta walk everywhere and spend as many nights outdoors as you can, stay in one place long enough to know it like the back of your hand, like your lover. I stripped myself of everything to be out there—out there!—and the problem with being out there is that then it is not *out there* anymore. It is more like *in here*. It can still be shockingly beautiful, and occasionally profound, but it is not the stuff of wonder because it lacks newness. The horizon might call to me, but I know too well how much food is in my pack, how far there is to travel, how much elevation there is to gain, how many miles my feet will tolerate before they rebel. I know too danged much. I will be working on the trail, clearing brush, say, and I'll see backpackers and recognize the glint in their eyes: the horizon beckons and promises redemption. If they are truly starstruck, I'll presume that they have read some books, the same ones I've read, Edward Abbey maybe or John Muir, and that they are being graced by the same wave of euphoria I had at nine in Minnesota. Here it is! Here it is! And I am happy for them. Then I get back to work. I check my watch: six more hours of hacking at the overgrown thimbleberry before quitting time. Don't get me wrong. I love where I work. I am humbled by the place, nurtured by it—*spoiled* by it, I know—and I wouldn't want to be anyplace else. But you can't be made new at home. So, in November, when trail work slows to a stop and clouds creep down the steep valley walls to settle somewhere near my eyebrows, it's time to get out.

Winter driving began, for me, when I left California for college in Oregon and began to zipper the West Coast: home for holidays then back to school. The advice my mother gave me for driving in the snow was this: Don't sweat it. There would be chain installers, she told me, and it would be worth twenty bucks to have someone else put them on. So I resolutely ignored weather warnings, and when the first big storm hit, I looked around for the chain fairies. They were nowhere to be found. I tried my damnedest through a four-hour white knuckler but managed to let a broken tire chain beat a frying pan-sized hole in the side of my Toyota and to spin three-sixty in the middle of I-5, episodes that frightened me some but not nearly enough. Eventually I reached a roadblock where a highway patrolman announced gruffly that, with only one chain, I was not in accordance with the law. Even I knew that. I tried to explain my predicament. He had no sympathy. Either put a chain on or turn around, he said. Turning around would mean risking my life all over again. Even I knew that. So I pulled a shoelace off one of my tennis shoes and tied the broken chain into place long enough to get past the roadblock and into a small town where the line of cars waiting to have chains repaired stretched as far as I could see. I parked and wandered into the tire shop to find a bathroom. There I noticed the shop owner confronting two young Mexican boys with a huge American truck. What do you want? he hollered. They mumbled in Spanish. Well, I interrupted, using my clumsy language skills, they want tire chains. (Duh!) The shop owner set them up and moved me to the front of the line. With hindsight, I'm not sure if it was an act of gratitude or pity—the hole in the Toyota was attracting a fair bit of derision already—but because of the shop owner's kindness, because of the whole ordeal, I decided there was adventure in winter travel. I needed a scolding, but I got encouragement.

❧

I was hooked. The off-chain hotels rarely cost more than thirty-five dollars a night, and the desk clerks were unfailingly friendly. The rooms were decorated a decade or three shy of fashion, with no cable TV, no bathtub, but there was a grocery store within walking distance or a diner where I could order a tuna melt, always a tuna melt, and a bottomless cup of coffee. The remnants of tourist season hung in the windows of closed shops: turquoise jewelry, buffalo beltbuckles, billboard ballcaps, fishing lures. Over the years, the towns, the routes, even the stops would become the same: the Thai restaurant in Alturas refashioned from an A&W drive-in, the motel in Lakeview with the armchairs upholstered exactly the same as my grandfather's. Sisters, Oregon. Monticello, Utah. Wisdom, Montana. The towns were near pretty places, but not too near.

It was, for me, a whole new America. In southern California in the hot pink eighties absolutely everything seemed artificial. I visited the Magic Kingdom thirty-seven times before I turned nineteen, and by then I craved something, anything, that would be the antithesis of Disney, the real thing. That's what I found on the highway: places you can count on, places where in the morning, without fail, there will be coffee at the gas station heading out of town—the smaller the town or the worse the roads, the fresher the coffee and the earlier it's made. And coffee doesn't make itself. On the edges of those miraculous untrammeled places were people who seemed, well, similarly unscathed. They were honest, if quirky, and unexpectedly generous, and they lived an ethic that the land itself, no matter how pretty, can't teach. It's an ethic so plain and unassuming, I can hardly say it without feeling, well, smarmy, but I'll say it anyhow: The Golden Rule.

⌒᷅

Then I met Laurie, and we drove everywhere without a thought, between jobs when we had no address, and after that even; even when we would rent a cheap apartment planning to hole up for the unpaid months, we never stayed too long at a stretch. Once we drove from Missoula, Montana, to the Olympic coast, a fourteen-hour drive over rutted ice, for a four-day backpacking trip. From Arizona, we drove regularly to Colorado to be surrounded by mountains. We drove daily even when we were home, wherever that was, in search of snow. Though we were not downhill skiers usually (we scorned the chairlifts, the groomed runs, mostly because we could not afford them), we cross-country skied often, anywhere, plodding through heavy sticky snow, over bare patches of dirt, across creeks and drainage ditches, then back to the car to put on the chains if need be and drive home.

Driving was comfort. I injured my knee one winter and saw an orthopedist who offered to schedule surgery to "sort things out." I wanted no part of it. What do you want to do? Laurie pleaded. I was crying. Well, have you ever seen Canada? Laurie asked. I had not! We drove north in blowing snow past, impossibly, a highway sign for a town named Riverside, the same as my orange-grove hometown in California. I considered stopping to wipe the snow off the sign to make it readable enough to take a snapshot, but we kept driving, snow funneling, headlight-lit, toward the windshield. By the time we reached the border and settled into a musty motel room in Osoyoos, I collected the sense to call my doctor back in Eugene, Oregon, who talked me into driving sixteen hours south, retracing our route and then some, for a more expert diagnosis.

And driving was necessity. For several years, we had to connect the dots of summer and winter employment: across eastern Washington, farmlands frozen hard and glittering in the sun, and over the mountains into Montana and south, farther and farther from the interstate as the temperature dropped to thirty below, then forty, through Yellowstone crowded with snow-cloaked bison, south through Idaho, empty Idaho, through Salt Lake City, sprawling and cosmopolitan, to the orange moonscape canyons of Utah, or through Nevada, even emptier, lots creepier, to the flat yellow saguaro deserts of Phoenix, to Laurie's grandma's tiny air-conditioned single-wide and many hands of gin rummy.

Eventually, predictably, it began to grow old. The motels grew more shabby, less quaint. We stayed in noisy rooms and filthy ones, rooms without hot water or phone service, rooms too hot or too cold, rooms furnished with surreal set-in-place fast-food furniture. We stayed in rooms normally occupied by full-time residents who pounded on the bolted door in the middle of the night, demanding we get the hell out. We shared one room with friends and discovered too late that it was, apparently, infested with wasps; we drugged ourselves with Benadryl and slept fitfully rather than try to find shelter elsewhere. Not infrequently we chose to shiver in the back of the pickup.

My inner-adult began to get the upper hand. Driving was costly and wasteful and unnecessarily dangerous, she'd remind me. Why can't you be more Annie Dillard and less Jackson Browne? she chided. More *Pilgrim at Tinker Creek*. And (this really hurt) no more *Running on Empty*. She eventually had to get her way.

So, we did it. We bought land, shackling ourselves with the mortgage payments in an unspeakably beautiful valley, and we drove north, one last time, from Arizona with a full U-Haul trailer. I had a persistent cold, as I often did during those moves, evidence that I was no longer enamored of the *On the Road* bit. I coughed and spit phlegm into a bandanna, while Laurie drove the overloaded truck dragging the trailer up through Nevada in a head wind so strong we could not go faster than forty. We stopped at a hilltop casino where icy wind gusted and where I drank tea to soothe my raw throat while we listened to the bells and buzzers of video poker. Then we stopped at a motel where Chevy Chase's *Las Vegas Vacation* played on cable, and we ate instant soup heated by hot tap water, and I thought I had never seen such a funny movie, that I had never been so happy. In two more days we would arrive in the tiny shack where we would stay for three years, saving money to build a bigger place.

That's how the story has to end, isn't it? You leave and gain perspective and then come home. There's comfort in comfort, the circle complete. You sow your wild oats terrorizing normal purposeful drivers from winter-savvy states like North Dakota or Wyoming. Then you settle down. I can sit here inside the new big house, snug with my tea and my cat and my memories, then when I have to travel, I can go by plane. It is faster and nearly as cheap as driving, right? And, as everyone tells me when they hear that I am a tad phobic, it is much safer. I can go to the airport, sterile and stuffy and overpriced, and even though I will never, ever, find a tuna melt on the menu, I can buy a magazine, the *New Yorker*, say, and tell myself to get used to it: *this* is the real world I craved so badly. My clothes and my speech and my rumpled duffel bags might seem shabby and out of fashion there, but such is the price of middle age. I will think I ought to make more money. I will sit in the too-cramped airplane seat, waiting for take-off with palms sweating, and regret all the things I should have done or been: a lawyer, a doctor, an engineer. I will fidget at cruising altitude and wait for the drinks to come around and before I know it, before I can even control myself, I'll start to long for the winter highway where you don't need a national emergency to pull people together, only a thick fog or some freezing rain, where people seem of a species, driving old vehicles that eke out the last fumes of gas seventies style, or trucks that gobble it up as if they have tapeworms, misfits every one. Oh it's useless.

The truth is I am not so old or settled. The truth is the allure of the road started to flag, sure, but it did not quite go away. Maybe if I had stayed at it longer or if I had to do it as a job, probably even if I had to do it in summer, the sheen would have worn off. As it is, I can't let go. I cling desperately the promise of the horizon that, due to the weather and my own skepticism, I can rarely even see. I can live with the fact that I don't believe in Disney or even Thoreau anymore, but by god I gotta draw the line. It's a little tiny thing, a distraction, romanticized all out of proportion, I know, but I gotta do it. I can't let the story end.

ⒸꙄ

Last weekend we hit the road. We drove a thousand miles south to my brother's apartment in Berkeley for Thanksgiving and tried to do it up right. We paid for a hotel room and spent our good stay-put wages like good Americans, and enjoyed the city, the shops, the family. On the way home, the weather turned sour. The interstate was jammed with holiday travelers and portable neon warnings flashed that chains would be required over the Siskiyous, so before dark we decided wisely, uncharacteristically, to stop for the night. We checked the big-name chain hotels by the freeways where travelers queued up dialing their cell phones in one lobby to call the next, trying to find an open room. Then we came to our senses. We drove down the old strip, deserted while the big-name places filled, and found a thirty-dollar room with disco furniture and a king-sized bed, a bathtub, and covered parking. We watched the local holiday parade replayed on television, then we walked down the empty parade-littered streets with tiny snowflakes skittering past signs for hardware stores and insurance offices. A few blocks south, nearer to the highway, we could see more intrepid travelers buying gas and chains and Snickers bars, forging ahead. In the morning we stopped for gas before daylight, filled travel mugs with piping hot Folgers, and hurried toward the onramp. I sipped my coffee and watched clouds skirt the foothills, splotchy with new snow. I listened to a public radio station broadcasting from a hundred miles off. When it came time, I crouched in my city clothes and fumbled with icy fingers to fasten the tighteners in place. Through the heavy slush, I could see a man approaching, ghostlike, with a huge number taped to his chest like a sled dog musher.

"Need help with your chains?" he asked. A bona fide chain installer he was, the first I had ever seen, and I would have paid the guy twenty bucks gladly, I wanted to tell him, twenty years earlier, but he came too late. We were ready to drive.

Everywhere But Here

⚜

When, a few years back, an ill-fated climber on Mt. Everest called his wife from near the summit, he changed, once and for all, the way people view telephones. Telephones became certifiably ubiquitous, not just in the home, but anywhere, everywhere. Everywhere, that is, but here.

I don't have a phone, not because I choose not to, but because I can't. The difference is that while the climber was on top of something I live at the bottom. Until recently, the mountains that hem this valley were too tall for a signal to navigate without a repeater, and the landowner, the National Park Service, maintains the same strict policy nationwide regarding repeaters in wilderness: there will be none. So, with a few notable exceptions, no one here has a telephone. It is occasionally inconvenient, yes, but it is remarkably peaceful. No telemarketers at dinner time. No interrupted projects or naps. No ever-present mental list of calls to make, calls to return, calls to dread receiving. Phonelessness is, very nearly, a state of grace. Predictably, it may be about to end.

Satellite technology has existed for a while that allows a signal to skip the repeater altogether and travel instead twenty-four thousand miles into space and back down to earth, but it has so far remained too expensive for most folks to afford. Times, alas, are changing. Last summer a small businessman quietly arrived in the valley offering to provide phones to every home for a cost of about eighteen dollars a month, an investment on which he may quietly receive healthy subsidies in money collected from phone customers in more populated areas. (It's not welfare, the businessman assures us, because it's not government money.) Only problem is, because extensive digging will be required to place fiber optic cable underground to carry the signal house-to-house once it bounces down from the heavens, regulators require a minimum number of commitments before service can be hooked up. That has brought this tiny community of about one hundred year-round residents to a singular dilemma: whether communally to decide not to have an amenity that much of the world has had for over a century.

The dilemma—the fact that we even consider it to be one—places us on the far end of a spectrum, out on the fringe with those who eye progress with no small measure of distrust. This is the vast landscape where bedraggled technophobes meet Luddites meet suburbanites driving Subarus with earnest bumper stickers: Live Simply So Others May Simply Live—those who swoon, secretly, when the typewriter key slaps, stiff-armed, against the page, those who use the drive-thru bank teller, still, and listen to cassette tapes, those who sit head-scratching through hip ads for Olympian cyberproducts. Faster! Higher! Stronger! Our discomfort is motivated by equal parts fear of the unknown and fear of divine punishment. Surely the gods will not tolerate this hubris much longer.

Meanwhile, at the other end of the spectrum, the true believers sit smugly with their genetically engineered dinner salads and cloned housepets preaching the unquestioned benevolence of it all. We ignore them, the enthusiasts, largely because they are so brash, because they feign to know so much more about it all—as if *how* to use it would, if we could only understand it, make perfectly clear *why*—and mostly because they seem to have missed the point. We clutter our lives with noisy buzzing contraptions, not because we believe the contraptions will make life on planet earth better in the long run, but because they might make life right here today, the toil of it, a little easier. We might choose to buy alarms to protect us from each other, or phones to connect us to each other, or wrist watches to get us home in time to fix supper, but we refuse to attend this mandatory pep rally—More! Newer! Better!—if for no other reason than that we remember the mushroom cloud. Technology is not, after all, morally neutral.

So here we are, the misfits, left to splitting hairs instead of atoms. I'll take the CD player but not the MP3, the microwave but not the Cuisinart, the ATM but not the online checking account. Each decision is dictated less by philosophy than by our pocketbooks and our tolerance for the eternal learning curve, the sheer humiliation of begging the fourteen-year-old again to set the VCR to record. (The VCR, not the DVD, we insist, trying futilely to draw the line even as the VHS is carted off to the landfill to join the BETA and the eight-track and the Atari.) Guilt and humility and frustration enter our homes uninvited with the so-called conveniences that leave us, in the end, fed up, burnt out, incapable of saying anything except this: Enough. Which brings us back to this tiny mountain town.

Our anti-phone crusade limps forward. There have been public meetings, letters written, and some grassroots organizing by unlikely bedfellows: staunch environmentalists and religious conservatives. Of course, not everyone is opposed to the idea. Rumor has it that one neighbor called requesting service to set the ball in motion, and the arguments in favor of getting telephones are rock solid and common as dirt: improved safety through faster contact with emergency medical personnel (though how they will get here any faster has yet to be determined), improved connection with family and friends whose closeness fades incrementally as people grow less apt to write letters the old-fashioned way. And, of course, there's business. It's hard enough to make a living in a remote tourist area without a handicap that precludes ATMs and makes accepting credit cards prohibitively risky. Local business owners want phones badly, and I can't say I blame them a bit.

The problem is, with this proposal at least, it can't be an individual decision. If there are enough commitments—right now it looks like there are—and phone service comes to the valley, nearly everyone agrees that it will become as difficult, as bizarre, as culturally ostracizing not to have a phone here as it is anywhere else.

"Once the cat's out of the bag," as one neighbor put it at a public meeting, "it's not going back in."

One way or the other, we are all in this together.

So the telephone opponents stand tall in the face of newspaper photographers who revel in the chance to capture the backwoodsy charm of this peculiar little skirmish, and they outline their points. Phones will allow people to move here who wouldn't otherwise, they say. Property taxes will rise exponentially. I am not convinced. This isolated valley is a long way from anywhere, and it is gorgeous beyond reason. The place is as likely to change people as they are to change it. I am not as worried about the people who might come as I am about those of us who are already here. We'll be compromised a little more, distracted a little longer, kept apart from the outdoors, apart from one another, apart as long as we possibly can, always, from our own silent unadorned selves.

Some people say that this debate is too little too late, that if we wanted our own little Shangri-La we ought to have stopped progress before electricity arrived here in the 1960s, before they paved the one road through town.

"It's like the *Titanic*. We're already going down," one neighbor told me. "This whole debate is over rearranging the deck furniture."

Of course rearranging our collective deck furniture is no new concept. It could very well be the theme, environmentally speaking, of the last half of the twentieth century. The Wilderness Act represented a last-ditch attempt to preserve the dregs, the hard-to-get-to remnants of virgin America, the plain lousiness of which, economically speaking, was conveniently masked in natural beauty. Wilderness preservation was symbolic—too little too late for the sequestered ecosystems, scientists now attest—but important for the increasingly urbanized American who needed to feel that someplace untrammeled still existed. The chosen tracts were to "generally appear to have been affected primarily by the forces of nature," the Act specified. There would be no roads in wilderness, no commercial activities, and no motorized equipment.

When I worked for the U.S. Forest Service, the nit-picking dictated by that phrase—"motorized equipment"—seemed to me the worst kind of frivolous dogma I'd ever encountered. (This despite a Catholic education). This is craziness! we exclaimed while we struggled with the crosscut saw, what old-timers call, understandably, a "misery whip." What is so inherently wrong with a chainsaw? We could save the government money. We could save ourselves from tendonitis. When I was deep in the woods, bandaging blisters, I could work myself into frenzy of resentment: wilderness preservation was a farce, I thought, an exercise in power by and for the elite, a Never Never Land for weekend refugees from the city. I'd yank again on the handle of the crosscut embedded three feet deep in a Douglas fir. Pure madness!

Only when we stumbled back down the trail after camping for the week, plodding giddily, exhausted, toward the wilderness boundary, did I appreciate the gesture. Through the trees, I could see the stubbly logged-out mountainsides that butted against the pristine and spread for miles. Standing on that imaginary line where the dregs meet the empty cup, where Never Never Land meets Weyerhaeuser, where absurdity meets decimation, I had to readjust my thinking. Later, after we were showered and fed, the debate would inevitably erupt in the bunkhouse all over again: Why? Why won't they let us? And I would remain silent. I understood the arguments, but I knew even then—even though I'd end up working trails for the National Park Service where chainsaws are the unquestioned and inarguably efficient norm—that given the choice I'd take absurdity. Every time.

This telephone debate is, if nothing else, absurd. For one thing, the valley already has a handful of phones: a couple of businesses have radio phones, and because the no-repeater policy applies only to commercial operations, nine years ago the Park Service installed a repeater and a multi-line satellite phone system in the ranger station. They also dedicated one line for valley residents and visitors. For now, if I want to make a telephone call, I drive six miles and, usually, wait in line to sit in a dirty graffiti-coated booth, home to the public phone. The connection is poor, hindered by a long satellite delay during which the least interruption by either party turns into dead air space. Receptionists often hang up in exasperation. Friends grumble in frustration.

But I'm not complaining. The satellite phone has become an acceptable way to deal with the business of life, just as having no phone at all seemed normal enough before then. Besides, not having a telephone at home comes with benefits. When neighbors have something to say, they stop by, and vice versa. We live in tenuous harmony here in our makeshift Shangri-La—liberals and conservatives, Christians and heathens, plain old-fashioned eccentrics—in part because we have to speak face-to-face.

Of course, the biggest reasons for not having phones aren't the advantages we gain, but the mind clog we avoid. When I go to the city, which I do often enough, I start off excited, clutching a fistful of lists and driving in concentric circles through priorities (change the oil, renew the permit, update the membership) and delicious distractions (bagels and lattes, hair salons and hardware megastores) amidst the radio ads, the billboards, the news, the music, the fashion on the street. No matter how I remind myself that it's my skewed perspective, my privileged situation, my defensive insecurity, perhaps, about the sacrifices I make to live where I do, the cacophony eventually drains me. By late afternoon, I am overwhelmed, defeated. If it's partly culture shock, my own self-inflicted problem, it is also sensory overload, real and common as the throbbing temple headache it invariably brings on. I head home. There, away from the commotion, I settle into the ordinary tasks of living—going to work, cooking food, doing laundry— reveling in the space and the silence, in the chance *not* to think.

The telephone, you see now, is not the problem, but the unwitting scapegoat, the last straw for those of us spouting the tired old complaint about busyness and the astonishing speed of twenty-first-century America. This whole dilemma is passé, the cynic in me concedes—so '70 s, so *Tao of Pooh*, so *Little House on the Prairie*. Besides, the whole mind-clog point is moot because the public phone isn't all we have. The Internet arrived sometime last year, and embracing that technology was an easier decision, a non-decision, because each household could choose for itself. There is no infrastructure, no subsidy, just a dish (albeit an expensive one, at about seventy dollars a month) on the side of the house. Nearly all the year-round residences has a dish, and already it's changing the way we deal with one another. The other day a seven-year-old girl walked three miles to a neighbor's house to visit. How will your mother know you're here? the neighbor asked. I can e-mail her, the girl replied. Duh! The kids are on the forefront, unquestioning. They scoff at their parents' ignorance, at their ambivalence, and they cling to the buddies they've made on instant messaging.

Laurie and I held off for a while, but eventually succumbed. I know the Internet is no better than the phone, and it may be worse—offering more gaudy flashing opportunities to part with your money than anything since Vegas—but Internet access saves me time and gas because I'm not driving up and down the valley to deliver messages or to use the public phone. I've driven five thousand miles in the past two years on essentially seven miles of road. It's mind boggling. It's humbling. Why not do it online? This is how change encroaches. One justification at a time.

Yesterday the sun peeked over the ridge tops for the first time since November, and I sat in front of the house, face upturned, against all the advice of dermatologists, craving it, desperate and elated. Awhile later, I stepped back in to type on my laptop, but my eyes could not adjust, so I put on my sunglasses. Through them, the screen appeared black, metaphorical. I could see everything else in the room, however dim, but the polarized lenses filtered the LCD as glare, superfluous and distracting. Like I don't already know that.

It's an awkward place to be, teetering on this edge, because our motives are so varied and so imperfect: isolationist, nostalgic, elitist. Most often, I feel self-conscious, embarrassed by our telephone quandary. Everywhere But Here seems a too-close cousin of Not in My Backyard. Fine for everyone else to navigate the labyrinthine reality of modern life replete with its instant gratification benefits and its migraine costs, we seem to say, but we're special. We'll take the good, but hold the bad. Buy the lumber, but boycott the clear-cut. Use the poison, but ship the waste someplace else. By opposing phone service we are designating ourselves as, well, a sort of wilderness. Living without amenities may not be an enviable lifestyle, but like the economically useless granite peaks that tower overhead, it is, for some people, a thing to be admired. This kind of idealization, precarious and entirely unrealistic, embarrasses me, frankly, more than the quandary itself, but I bring it up because it suggests the only argument that eases my conscience: we're not only doing this for ourselves.

Visitors who flock here by the thousands in summer drawn by the natural beauty often decide at some point that they need to make a telephone call. After waiting in line for an hour at the public phone or after being cut off repeatedly by the lousy connection, they decide they don't need to make the call that badly after all. You can see it on their faces—exasperation, then exultation. Free at last! Free at last! They've discovered the secret of the skewed perspective: that phone calls are almost never urgent, that hardly anything is. We don't need phones, none of us do, and maybe, self-congratulatory and absurdly symbolic as it may be, it's worth it to be the one place without them.

Still, the teenagers stand in our faces, taller than we are and more sure of themselves, and they say what teenagers always say: Why? Or in this case: Why not? At a dinner party recently, the parents of a thirteen-year-old bragged that the boy could instant message and reply to e-mail and play complicated computer games all at once, that he'd been wired at a new, faster speed than we had. It wasn't much different, I suppose, from my mother marveling twenty years ago that I could listen to rock music and do homework at the same time when I couldn't explain to her that sometimes I couldn't concentrate *without* the music. I could see it when the thirteen-year-old rolled his eyes. Gawd! It's no big deal. And I wished I had the vocabulary to ask him about space and silence. I wished he had the vocabulary to answer. I want to side with youth, truly. I'm drawn to their vibrancy—they are strong and smart, curious and discerning—and I'm seduced by their enthusiasm, but I am old enough, just barely, to know the failure of this seduction. They don't know what they're losing. They never do.

I can feel it coming now, the loss of innocence, subtle and insistent as a rip tide. We're going down. Of course, I'm not saying it's wrong to get telephones. I grew up with a telephone. I use the public phone regularly. Guilty as charged. All I am saying is that it is awfully sad to think that here we are, one of the last places in these technologically burdened United States with the chance to say "No"—to something, to anything—and to think that we might let that chance slip away. The telephone is one step too far, and if kids get to accept everything, I can hoard the right to refuse this one thing, if for no other reason than because the unscathed idealist in me believes in it, the refusing. We're not fooling with the deck furniture. We're playing music while we sink. It's not gonna make a bit of difference, probably, but it's strangely beautiful, and liberating as hell to say it, finally, to get to say it for everyone who can't: Here's where it stops. Enough. I have better things not to think about.

Near the Mountains

I was sent to the west side of the park early this spring, before the snow had melted off the trails, before I normally would have any reason to work. Despite the paycheck, I took the assignment as banishment and whined considerably. The west side, the wet side, receives about 120 inches of rain a year. Most of it seems to come in March. The only advantage would be the chance to see some people I had known a few years earlier, before I abandoned the rich and loamy for dust and pines.

The barn that serves as trail headquarters in Marblemount was blandly unchanged. Hand tools—shovels, sledgehammers, axes, hand drills—and horse equipment crowded spider-webbed corners. The smell of musty hay mingled with baked-on coffee. Rain spattered on the roof continually. The line of cars parked in the gravel out front averaged fifteen years old.

The trail crew straggled in somber and familiar as the setting, wearing Levis and logging boots, oil-stained wool shirts, suspenders. They greeted me warmly. How was your winter? How is so-and-so? Good. Good. Hugs. Then we settled into gathering equipment for the day. While they stuffed sandwiches and rain gear into battered daypacks and argued over the merits of one boot grease over another, I shyly noted the changes since I'd seen them last. Thicker forearms. Deeper calluses. More scars. It should be no surprise, I told myself. It's not as if the work hasn't changed me, too.

When I first worked on the west side of the Cascades, I was twenty-three, injured, working as a dispatcher in the fire office. I'd done my stint as a volunteer. I'd discovered the North Cascades, spent a summer on the east side, fallen in love, and promptly torn my knee to pieces on an ill-advised ski trip. Then I'd landed on the west side, on Laurie's heels, in the whirlwind that was our life, and I was glad as hell to have a job. I was glad as hell just to be there. Even though I was cooped up inside, even though I was as far from my sunny California roots as I could possibly be, there was Romance in the air with a capital R—the slow rhythms of plants growing steadily, incessantly, tall and lush, the clouds rolling in off the Pacific and settling snug against the knife-edged peaks and raining, raining, raining, and mostly, the promise of the high country, inaccessible by car, but out there still. Right out there! Beyond the pasture and the trails barn, on a clear day, you could see summits and false summits, the endless stretch of nameless ridges that framed the horizon like so many broken pieces of glass imbedded in a stucco wall. I could feel the closeness of those mountains even through the fog, even as I sat at the computer listening to Jerry Jeff Walker on a monophonic tape player from Kmart, watching condensation drip from single-paned windows, and waiting until two o'clock when the backcountry rangers stationed at lookouts would call in their daily fire weather reports.

"Sixty-eight," they might say. "Partly cloudy."

I could picture it up there. Cloud shadows skating across the heather-cloaked meadows. Occasional sun illuminating the remaining snow on the north slopes. I could hear in the rangers' voices that they knew they were lucky. I knew it, too. I knew they would spend their days walking for miles along narrow ridgeline trails crowded by huckleberries growing ripe by the hour, by tiny subalpine firs fighting for unclaimed ground. I knew they'd spend their evenings writing in the lookout log books long heartfelt tributes to the mountains or to the writers who had been stationed there before: Kerouac, Snyder. I had way too much time to think about it.

Even so—even though I would have given my eye teeth to be perched above the trees reliving Snyder's spirituality, Kerouac's hyperbole—I knew that backcountry rangering wasn't for me. The young backcountry rangers—most of them were around my age— took their jobs a bit too seriously, as if being above the trees so much of the time they considered themselves above other things. Like work. So busy were the rangers hiking and enforcing rules that they didn't often have to get dirty. I didn't want to be above anything. I wanted to be dirty, filthy even.

The trail crew was dirty. Every other Tuesday they would hang around the barn, packing up for their eight-day hitch. To pass the time, they'd loiter in the fire office, sifting through ancient military-issue Meals Ready to Eat, picking out the Tabasco sauce or the brownie. I'd ask about where they were headed, what their projects would be, and plain green envy must have shown on my face. On one of those mornings, after the crew had left, one of the supervisors tried to distract me.

"If you could have any job in the park," he asked, "what would it be?"

"Trail crew," I answered.

He groaned.

"You seemed so smart," he said. He recounted stories of the trail crew—dumb, every last one of them—carrying too-heavy packs. He described the injuries: gory impalements, back surgeries. He fell silent for a moment as I answered a radio call, then continued his litany: gruesome deaths with cables and ropes, falls, drownings, plain mysterious disappearances. I was grateful for the company, but I didn't listen. The next year my knee was completely recovered, and I went to work on a trail crew.

Back on the west side this spring, I crowded into a tool-strewn Suburban, and we crept out through town in a drizzle. Marblemount, like Darrington, or even Stehekin, is not, technically, in the mountains, certainly not like some of those Colorado towns are—Leadville, say, or Aspen. It sits at low elevation, nearly sea level, more in the trees—the second- and third-growth hemlock and fir, alder and maple—than it is in the mountains. The sign driving out of town reads *Last Tavern for 89 Miles*. That tavern was itself closed for most of the three years I lived over there. The place sported a neon sign to prove it: *Closed*.

"Lousy day," Mike, the driver, mumbled.

"Yea, gawd, it gets worse. I ever tell you about the time I was in a Mexican jail?" Smitty drawled the story opener in a New Jersey accent. He sucked coffee from a plastic mug laced tight in the cutoff top of a logger's boot. "Heh. Heh. You talk about lousy."

I had seen the mug/boot years before when Smitty would hang around the fire office with the others. I had admired him then for his obvious strength and skill, and mainly for his stories, for the story his life had become. He'd graduated from a Catholic prep school back East and moved West. Twenty-five years he'd lived in the Skagit Valley. Like most of his neighbors, he was part-redneck, part-hippie, and a whole lot more than either: a certified EMT with the volunteer fire department, a skilled mountaineer, a former logger who'd been married twice and built his own home, raised goats and mules and chickens and a couple of kids. Over the years, he and his wife had housed dozens of idealistic kids traveling through the valley, working for the Park Service, or on local organic farms, or teaching environmental education classes for sixth-graders. Supposedly, Smitty's mug/boot was not affectation, but a makeshift splint in case of a medical emergency.

"I was drunk, like I was always drunk, sleeping in some arroyo, you know, just outside town when the *federales* find me. They wanna see my papers and I don't have no stinkin' papers."

Mike, the driver, laughed.

"You like that movie, Smitty?"

"What movie?"

I remember Mike from before, too, from when he was a handsome college kid working his summers in the woods. Even then he was the intellectual on the crew, though his manners have always kept him from flaunting the fact. Later in the week, when we are alone in the truck, Mike will discuss feminist literary theorists and changing historical perspectives on the Holocaust. Then, even later in the week, he will admit to feeling as though he's wasting his life on trails, that he ought to finish his PhD, teach at the very least, or do something of value, something real. He drops the reference to *Treasure of the Sierra Madre* and lets Smitty hog center stage.

"So, they say, what about money? *Dinero,* comprenday? I comprendayed, but I sure as hell didn't have any money left, so I acted stupid, and that didn't work a bit. They locked me up."

We meandered east along the Skagit, churning now through a narrow gorge, then past Seattle City Light's three massive hydroelectric dams, dodging rocks that plummet regularly from the blasted roadcuts threatening to shatter your windshield or worse. Then, finally, we were in the mountains.

"Well, Smitty, how was it?" Karen finally asked with more than a hint of skepticism. A serious climber and a sometimes Outward Bound instructor, Karen could probably tell a few stories of her own. But bravado is not in her nature. Like me, Karen has worked for many years as the only woman on all male crews. She suffers neither fools nor lies gladly.

Smitty grinned and rolled his eyes devilishly. "You wouldn't want to know."

We parked at the trailhead and walked a mile along a wide spring-swelled creek to the worksite—a long stretch of tread undermined by erosion. Once there we set ourselves at positioning rocks as a crib to hold the trail. Working in pairs, we pried with rock bars and set up come-alongs, talking through the process.

"Try setting the choker on the far side to get it to roll."

"OK, and then I'll get the bar under it to get it started."

The rocks were large and unwieldy. The drizzle was incessant. The work was slow and tiring and frankly boring, and I wished for a while with all my might that I were still laid off. I looked around at the others. Surely they felt the same way. We came to the mountains for one reason: to be there. Right out there! Now we stayed for a hundred reasons, I thought. For the security. For the kids. To squirrel away cash for the next big climb in the Andes or the Himalayas. To pay the tuition, or in my case, the mortgage. Sometimes, I reminded myself, it's just a paycheck.

"You gonna give me a hand here or not?" Smitty called, and I left my reverie.

Toward the end of the day, we needed to backfill with smaller rock from a talus field at the far end of the cribbing. We shoveled into five-gallon buckets, then walked quickly, silent now, not much to work out about shoveling. Mike began to walk faster. Not to be outdone, we all picked up the pace, faster, then faster yet, balancing on the talus at a trot with forty pounds of rock in each hand. As we did, the late-afternoon sky began to brighten, then to break apart until sunlight rebounded, brilliant and blinding, off of the creek below. I looked up at Mike, Smitty, and Karen filling their buckets with single-minded purpose. They were older than last time I'd seen them, sure, but steadfast and unfathomably stubborn. If glee is sometimes at a minimum on a trail crew, I thought, pride runs thick as moss.

⟅⟆

Truth is, Laurie and I left the west side after three years mainly because I couldn't hack it. I longed for sunlight. During fifteen-minute breaks, I would stumble over downed logs and crash through soaking brush to find a break in the canopy where I might warm myself briefly. The grommets on my boots began to rust. My wool pants never dried. Once I left my favorite shirt next to a log that we had been sawing out. I think of that shirt surprisingly often, never picturing the most likely end—that a deer chewed it to bits for the salt content. Instead I see it disintegrating until it is indistinguishable from the three or four feet of rotting duff on the forest floor. I figure the shirt was my offering to those drippy woods instead of myself. I got out. We moved back over the mountains— thirty miles as the crow flies—to where forty inches of precipitation is average and much of that comes in snow. Laurie and I bought our land and built our house and dug in our heels. What I couldn't figure out was why the rest of them stayed.

Some of the east-side trails I work these days are rutted troughs of loose dirt and rocks. When we scrape the berm back into the rut, dust coats our clothes a quarter-inch thick. There is no mud to be found. And it's not just the weather that's different. With chainsaws, the work moves faster, more predictably. How best to navigate the complex angles of suspended logs is decided in split-seconds. Orange plastic wedges remain more often in the side pocket of your gas-soaked pack as you become more adept at timing the undercut. What once seemed daunting now seems commonplace. I know. I know. It is maturity encroaching like an unwelcome curfew. You head out to the foreign places of youth, the places farthest from what you've been, to test the boundaries, and end up walking, impossibly, with a chainsaw resting on a scrap of horse blanket on your shoulder like an appendage. You walk for days, weeks, months along familiar stretches of trail that unfurl like lyrics to oldies tunes on the radio. (How do you know this? You don't remember learning this.) What was once strange and wondrous, you decide, is now the norm. You cut a few logs, refill the saw gas, and you walk some more. Then sometime in mid-summer, you reach it: the dustless, mudless high alpine meadows skirted by glaciers, glaciers everywhere. Then you are right in it, what you came for. It's not the sort of thing you ever want to call much attention to, like skiing the perfect run. ("Look. Look," you might want to say, "I'm doing it." Then inevitably you fall.) So you try to stay quiet, not to say to your coworkers: "Look where the holy heck we are." It would be embarrassing somehow, too touchy-feely, like a teenager telling her parents that she loves them.

↶

On the ride home from work, the mountains glowed pink in the fading sunlight. Between the aptly named peaks—Terror, Desolation, Forbidden—snowy ridges were spotlighted creamy, benign, so close and inviting. Mike, the driver and the skier, stared in awe, his eyes darting upwards from the curvy highway.

"Look at that," Mike said.

Yeah, yeah, we agreed in silence, but watch the danged road. I figured that would be where it stayed. After all, we know too well how far it is to those ridges, the technical skill required to reach them. Those are the kinds of places trails never reach. Trails are just approaches, mapped and constructed throughways. They are not, after all, destinations in themselves.

Up front Smitty feigned sleep, his head tucked in against his bunched-up shirt, leaning against the window. Another jag in the road jerked him awake.

"Look at that," he said. "Wouldn't you just love to go up there, maybe for week, stay spiked out? Gawd, it'd be nice, wouldn't it? I'm gonna get some of those new plastic ski boots. Where'd you say we could get those, Mike? I'm going to Vancouver this weekend. I'm gonna buy myself a pair and no taxes. Will you write it down again? Exactly which kind?"

"Sure," Mike said. "Sure."

"Then we can go up there and ski, all of us." Smitty looked around the rig.

We all nodded vaguely, gazing up dreamily and sharing in Smitty's rare spontaneous fit of camaraderie. I was surprised, and

I was pondering the growing respect it takes to live this way, with wilderness as very nearly—but not quite—home. The honeymoon passes, the hay grows musty, the calluses thick. Maybe we can't live in it, what we hope for, but we can live in the hope, driving precariously old vehicles on one-lane highways, weathering the weariness and the injuries, and well, the weather. I realized that of course I did know why they'd stayed all these years, the same reason I had—not for the mossy pride or the mortgage—but because east side or west side, this job, this life is full of Romance.

"Yeah," Smitty continued, "a sunny spring day like this, I'd be up there with my fleece jacket zipped down to the navel."

We stifled giggles, though it made a strange sort of sense. Sure, this isn't California or Colorado, not the sort of place to cavort without a coat. Still, there are moments, rare ones, when you might venture to unzip it.

"To the what?" Karen asked finally. "What did you say?"

"To the navel!" Smitty roared.

"To the navel!" Karen repeated in mock salute.

"To the navel!" Mike and I echoed.

We fell into hysterics, laughing as we descended back into the trees along the river, knowing tomorrow would likely bring rain, as would the next day and the next, watching the alpine glow fade, not even considering how very long it might be until we see it again.

Acknowledgements

Some of the essays in this collection have been previously published as follows:

"Children of the Woods." *Weber Studies*, Fall 2003.

"Everywhere But Here." *Orion*, July/Aug 2003.

"Long Distance." *Sport Literate*, Father's Issue 2003.

"Red Tape and Yellow Stickies." *Fine Homebuilding*, Spring/ Summer 2002.

"Now Go Home." *Open Spaces*: *Views from the Northwest*, Volume 3 Issue 2 2000.

"Doing Without." *Orion*, Winter 2000.

"The Doodles We Draw." *Stehekin Choice*, Autumn 1999.

"The Tourists in my Yard." *Talking River Review*, Winter 1998.

"Entombing Spiders and Other Small Shack Stories." *Stehekin Choice*, Autumn 1998.

"How to Waste Time." *Stehekin Choice*, Autumn 1997.

"Wilderness, Homelessness, and the Crosscut Saw." *Kinesis*, March 1997. First Prize in national "If It Moves" personal essay contest 1996.